DOVER·THRIFT·EDITIONS

Dover Beach and Other Poems

MATTHEW ARNOLD

DOVER PUBLICATIONS, INC.
New York

DOVER THRIFT EDITIONS

GENERAL EDITOR: STANLEY APPELBAUM
EDITOR OF THIS VOLUME: CANDACE WARD

Published in Canada by General Publishing Company, Ltd., 30 Lesmill Road, Don Mills, Toronto, Ontario.

Published in the United Kingdom by Constable and Company, Ltd., 3 The Lanchesters, 162–164 Fulham Palace Road, London W6 9ER.

Bibliographical Note

This Dover edition, first published by Dover Publications, Inc. in 1994, contains a new selection of 26 poems reprinted from a standard text. The Note and alphabetical lists of titles and first lines have been prepared specially for this volume.

Library of Congress Cataloging-in-Publication Data

Arnold, Matthew, 1822–1888.
    Dover Beach and other poems / Matthew Arnold.
      p.   cm. — (Dover thrift editions)
    "This Dover edition . . . contains a new selection of 26 poems reprinted from a standard text" — T.p. verso.
    Includes indexes.
    ISBN 0-486-28037-3 (pbk.)
    I. Title.   II. Series.
PR4022.D6   1994
821'.8 — dc20
                                                      93-23660
                                                         CIP

Manufactured in the United States of America
Dover Publications, Inc., 31 East 2nd Street, Mineola, N.Y. 11501

Note

MATTHEW ARNOLD was born December 24, 1822 at Laleham, on the Thames River. Son of Dr. Thomas Arnold, famous Head Master of Rugby School and educational reformer, Arnold became exposed at an early age to the combined influences of liberal studies and contemporary society. As a boy, Arnold spent many of his school holidays at Fox How, near Grasmere, where Nature, as Wordsworth knew it earlier in the century, also exercised a profound influence on him. In 1841 Arnold began his studies at Balliol College, Oxford, and in 1851 he was appointed Inspector of Schools, a position he maintained for 35 years.

Arnold's first two volumes of poetry appeared anonymously in 1849 (*The Strayed Reveller, and other Poems, by A.*) and 1852 (*Empedocles on Etna, and other Poems, by A.*). By 1853 Arnold was confident enough to publish his *Poems* under his full name. These initial volumes were followed in 1855 by *Poems, by Matthew Arnold, Second Series* and *New Poems* in 1867. In the 20 years that followed, however, Arnold wrote very little verse, spending most of his energies on the literary and social criticism, religious and educational writings for which he is equally famous. Whether in prose or poetry, Arnold's work reveals his acute sense of man's position in his society. Particularly in the poems, that position is one of alienation and isolation, as seen, for example, in "Stanzas from the Grande Chartreuse" and "Dover Beach." Writing in 1869, Arnold himself identified his verse as the representation of "the main movement of mind of the last quarter of a century," as a product of the social and historical forces of the mid-Victorian Age.

Contents

Dover Beach
and Other Poems

To a Friend

Who prop, thou ask'st, in these bad days, my mind?
He much, the old man, who, clearest-soul'd of men,
Saw The Wide Prospect, and the Asian Fen,
And Tmolus' hill, and Smyrna's bay, though blind.
Much he, whose friendship I not long since won,
That halting slave, who in Nicopolis
Taught Arrian, when Vespasian's brutal son
Clear'd Rome of what most sham'd him. But be his
My special thanks, whose even-balanc'd soul,
From first youth tested up to extreme old age,
Business could not make dull, nor Passion wild:
Who saw life steadily, and saw it whole:
The mellow glory of the Attic stage;
Singer of sweet Colonus, and its child.

The Forsaken Merman

Come, dear children, let us away;
Down and away below.
Now my brothers call from the bay;
Now the great winds shorewards blow;
Now the salt tides seawards flow;
Now the wild white horses play,
Champ and chafe and toss in the spray.
Children dear, let us away.
This way, this way.

Call her once before you go.
Call once yet.
In a voice that she will know:
"Margaret! Margaret!"
Children's voices should be dear
(Call once more) to a mother's ear:
Children's voices, wild with pain.
Surely she will come again.

Call her once and come away.
This way, this way.
"Mother dear, we cannot stay."
The wild white horses foam and fret.
"Margaret! Margaret!"

Come, dear children, come away down.
Call no more.
One last look at the white-wall'd town,
And the little grey church on the windy shore.
Then come down.
She will not come though you call all day.
Come away, come away.

Children dear, was it yesterday
We heard the sweet bells over the bay?
In the caverns where we lay,
Through the surf and through the swell,
The far-off sound of a silver bell?
Sand-strewn caverns, cool and deep,
Where the winds are all asleep;
Where the spent lights quiver and gleam;
Where the salt weed sways in the stream;
Where the sea-beasts rang'd all round
Feed in the ooze of their pasture-ground;
Where the sea-snakes coil and twine,
Dry their mail and bask in the brine;
Where great whales come sailing by,
Sail and sail, with unshut eye,
Round the world for ever and ay?
When did music come this way?
Children dear, was it yesterday?

Children dear, was it yesterday
(Call yet once) that she went away?
Once she sate with you and me,
On a red gold throne in the heart of the sea,
And the youngest sate on her knee.
She comb'd its bright hair, and she tended it well,
When down swung the sound of the far-off bell.
She sigh'd, she look'd up through the clear green sea.
She said; "I must go, for my kinsfolk pray

In the little grey church on the shore to-day.
'Twill be Easter-time in the world—ah me!
And I lose my poor soul, Merman, here with thee."
I said; "Go up, dear heart, through the waves.
Say thy prayer, and come back to the kind sea-caves."
She smil'd, she went up through the surf in the bay.
Children dear, was it yesterday?

    Children dear, were we long alone?
"The sea grows stormy, the little ones moan.
Long prayers," I said, "in the world they say.
Come," I said, and we rose through the surf in the bay.
We went up the beach, by the sandy down
Where the sea-stocks bloom, to the white-wall'd town.
Through the narrow pav'd streets, where all was still,
To the little grey church on the windy hill.
From the church came a murmur of folk at their prayers,
But we stood without in the cold blowing airs.
We climb'd on the graves, on the stones, worn with rains,
And we gaz'd up the aisle through the small leaded panes.
She sate by the pillar; we saw her clear:
"Margaret, hist! come quick, we are here.
Dear heart," I said, "we are long alone.
The sea grows stormy, the little ones moan."
But, ah, she gave me never a look,
For her eyes were seal'd to the holy book.
"Loud prays the priest; shut stands the door."
Come away, children, call no more.
Come away, come down, call no more.

    Down, down, down.
Down to the depths of the sea.
She sits at her wheel in the humming town,
Singing most joyfully.
Hark, what she sings; "O joy, O joy,
For the humming street, and the child with its toy.
For the priest, and the bell, and the holy well.
For the wheel where I spun,
And the blessed light of the sun."
And so she sings her fill,
Singing most joyfully,
Till the shuttle falls from her hand,

And the whizzing wheel stands still.
She steals to the window, and looks at the sand;
And over the sand at the sea;
And her eyes are set in a stare;
And anon there breaks a sigh,
And anon there drops a tear,
From a sorrow-clouded eye,
And a heart sorrow-laden,
A long, long sigh,
For the cold strange eyes of a little Mermaiden,
And the gleam of her golden hair.

Come away, away children.
Come children, come down.
The hoarse wind blows colder;
Lights shine in the town.
She will start from her slumber
When gusts shake the door;
She will hear the winds howling,
Will hear the waves roar.
We shall see, while above us
The waves roar and whirl,
A ceiling of amber,
A pavement of pearl.
Singing, "Here came a mortal,
But faithless was she.
And alone dwell for ever
The kings of the sea."

But, children, at midnight,
When soft the winds blow;
When clear falls the moonlight;
When spring-tides are low:
When sweet airs come seaward
From heaths starr'd with broom;
And high rocks throw mildly
On the blanch'd sands a gloom:
Up the still, glistening beaches,
Up the creeks we will hie;
Over banks of bright seaweed
The ebb-tide leaves dry.
We will gaze, from the sand-hills,
At the white, sleeping town;

At the church on the hill-side —
And then come back down.
Singing, "There dwells a lov'd one,
But cruel is she.
She left lonely for ever
The kings of the sea."

The Strayed Reveller

The Portico of Circe's Palace.   Evening.

A Youth.   Circe

THE YOUTH

Faster, faster,
O Circe, Goddess,
Let the wild, thronging train,
The bright procession
Of eddying forms,
Sweep through my soul!
Thou standest, smiling
Down on me; thy right arm
Lean'd up against the column there,
Props thy soft cheek;
Thy left holds, hanging loosely,
The deep cup, ivy-cinctur'd,
I held but now.

Is it then evening
So soon? I see, the night dews,
Cluster'd in thick beads, dim
The agate brooch-stones
On thy white shoulder.
The cool night-wind, too,
Blows through the portico,
Stirs thy hair, Goddess,
Waves thy white robe.

CIRCE

Whence art thou, sleeper?

THE YOUTH

When the white dawn first
Through the rough fir-planks
Of my hut, by the chestnuts,
Up at the valley-head,
Came breaking, Goddess,
I sprang up, I threw round me
My dappled fawn-skin:
Passing out, from the wet turf,
Where they lay, by the hut door,
I snatch'd up my vine-crown, my fir staff,
All drench'd in dew:
Came swift down to join
The rout early gather'd
In the town, round the temple,
Iacchus' white fane
On yonder hill.
Quick I pass'd, following
The wood-cutters' cart-track
Down the dark valley; — I saw
On my left, through the beeches,
Thy palace, Goddess,
Smokeless, empty:
Trembling, I enter'd; beheld
The court all silent,
The lions sleeping;
On the altar, this bowl.
I drank, Goddess —
And sunk down here, sleeping,
On the steps of thy portico.

CIRCE

Foolish boy! Why tremblest thou?
Thou lovest it, then, my wine?
Wouldst more of it? See, how glows,
Through the delicate flush'd marble,
The red creaming liquor,
Strown with dark seeds!
Drink, then! I chide thee not,

Deny thee not my bowl.
Come, stretch forth thy hand, then — so, —
Drink, drink again!

THE YOUTH

Thanks, gracious One!
Ah, the sweet fumes again!
More soft, ah me!
More subtle-winding
Than Pan's flute-music.
Faint — faint! Ah me!
Again the sweet sleep.

CIRCE

Hist! Thou — within there!
Come forth, Ulysses!
Art tired with hunting?
While we range the woodland,
See what the day brings.

ULYSSES

Ever new magic!
Hast thou then lur'd hither,
Wonderful Goddess, by thy art,
The young, languid-ey'd Ampelus,
Iacchus' darling —
Or some youth belov'd of Pan,
Of Pan and the Nymphs?
That he sits, bending downward
His white, delicate neck
To the ivy-wreath'd marge
Of thy cup: — the bright, glancing vine-leaves
That crown his hair,
Falling forwards, mingling
With the dark ivy-plants;
His fawn-skin, half untied,
Smear'd with red wine-stains? Who is he,
That he sits, overweigh'd
By fumes of wine and sleep,

So late, in thy portico?
What youth, Goddess, — what guest
Of Gods or mortals?

CIRCE

Hist! he wakes!
I lur'd him not hither, Ulysses.
Nay, ask him!

THE YOUTH

Who speaks? Ah! Who comes forth
To thy side, Goddess, from within?
How shall I name him?
This spare, dark-featur'd,
Quick-ey'd stranger?
Ah! and I see too
His sailor's bonnet,
His short coat, travel-tarnish'd,
With one arm bare. —
Art thou not he, whom fame
This long time rumours
The favour'd guest of Circe, brought by the waves?
Art thou he, stranger?
The wise Ulysses,
Laertes' son?

ULYSSES

I am Ulysses.
And thou, too, sleeper?
Thy voice is sweet.
It may be thou hast follow'd
Through the islands some divine bard,
By age taught many things,
Age and the Muses;
And heard him delighting
The chiefs and people
In the banquet, and learn'd his songs,
Of Gods and Heroes,
Of war and arts,
And peopled cities

Inland, or built
By the grey sea. — If so, then hail!
I honour and welcome thee.

THE YOUTH

The Gods are happy.
They turn on all sides
Their shining eyes:
And see, below them,
The Earth, and men.

They see Tiresias
Sitting, staff in hand.
On the warm, grassy
Asopus' bank:
His robe drawn over
His old, sightless head:
Revolving inly
The doom of Thebes.

They see the Centaurs
In the upper glens
Of Pelion, in the streams,
Where red-berried ashes fringe
The clear-brown shallow pools;
With streaming flanks, and heads
Rear'd proudly, snuffing
The mountain wind.

They see the Indian
Drifting, knife in hand,
His frail boat moor'd to
A floating isle thick matted
With large-leav'd, low-creeping melon-plants,
And the dark cucumber.
He reaps, and stows them,
Drifting — drifting: — round him,
Round his green harvest-plot,
Flow the cool lake-waves:
The mountains ring them.

They see the Scythian
On the wide Stepp, unharnessing

His wheel'd house at noon.
He tethers his beast down, and makes his meal,
Mares' milk, and bread
Bak'd on the embers: — all around
The boundless waving grass-plains stretch, thick-starr'd
With saffron and the yellow hollyhock
And flag-leav'd iris flowers.
Sitting in his cart
He makes his meal: before him, for long miles,
Alive with bright green lizards.
And the springing bustard fowl,
The track, a straight black line,
Furrows the rich soil: here and there
Clusters of lonely mounds
Topp'd with rough-hewn,
Grey, rain-blear'd statues, overpeer
The sunny Waste.

They see the Ferry
On the broad, clay-laden
Lone Chorasmian stream: thereon
With snort and strain,
Two horses, strongly swimming, tow
The ferry boat, with woven ropes
To either bow
Firm-harness'd by the mane: — a Chief,
With shout and shaken spear
Stands at the prow, and guides them: but astern,
The cowering Merchants, in long robes,
Sit pale beside their wealth
Of silk-bales and of balsam-drops,
Of gold and ivory,
Of turquoise-earth and amethyst,
Jasper and chalcedony,
And milk-barr'd onyx stones.
The loaded boat swings groaning
In the yellow eddies.
The Gods behold them.

They see the Heroes
Sitting in the dark ship
On the foamless, long-heaving,
Violet sea:

At sunset nearing
The Happy Islands.

These things, Ulysses,
The wise Bards also
Behold and sing.
But oh, what labour!
O Prince, what pain!

They too can see
Tiresias: — but the Gods,
Who give them vision,
Added this law:
That they should bear too
His groping blindness,
His dark foreboding,
His scorn'd white hairs.
Bear Hera's anger
Through a life lengthen'd
To seven ages.

They see the Centaurs
On Pelion: — then they feel,
They too, the maddening wine
Swell their large veins to bursting: in wild pain
They feel the biting spears
Of the grim Lapithae, and Theseus, drive,
Drive crashing through their bones: they feel
High on a jutting rock in the red stream
Alcmena's dreadful son
Ply his bow: — such a price
The Gods exact for song;
To become what we sing.

They see the Indian
On his mountain lake: — but squalls
Make their skiff reel, and worms
In the unkind spring have gnaw'd
Their melon-harvest to the heart: They see
The Scythian: — but long frosts
Parch them in winter-time on the bare Stepp,
Till they too fade like grass: they crawl
Like shadows forth in spring.

They see the Merchants
On the Oxus' stream: — but care
Must visit first them too, and make them pale.
Whether, through whirling sand,
A cloud of desert robber-horse has burst
Upon their caravan: or greedy kings,
In the wall'd cities the way passes through,
Crush'd them with tolls: or fever-airs,
On some great river's marge,
Mown them down, far from home.

They see the Heroes
Near harbour: — but they share
Their lives, and former violent toil, in Thebes,
Seven-gated Thebes, or Troy:
Or where the echoing oars
Of Argo, first,
Startled the unknown Sea.

The old Silenus
Came, lolling in the sunshine,
From the dewy forest coverts,
This way, at noon.
Sitting by me, while his Fauns
Down at the water side
Sprinkled and smooth'd
His drooping garland,
He told me these things.

But I, Ulysses,
Sitting on the warm steps,
Looking over the valley,
All day long, have seen,
Without pain, without labour,
Sometimes a wild-hair'd Maenad;
Sometimes a Faun with torches;
And sometimes, for a moment,
Passing through the dark stems
Flowing-rob'd — the belov'd,
The desir'd, the divine,
Belov'd Iacchus.

Ah cool night-wind, tremulous stars!
Ah glimmering water —

Fitful earth-murmur —
Dreaming woods!
Ah golden-hair'd, strangely-smiling Goddess,
And thou, prov'd, much enduring,
Wave-toss'd Wanderer!
Who can stand still?
Ye fade, ye swim, ye waver before me.
The cup again!

Faster, faster,
O Circe, Goddess,
Let the wild thronging train,
The bright procession
Of eddying forms,
Sweep through my soul!

Shakespeare

Others abide our question. Thou art free.
We ask and ask: Thou smilest and art still,
Out-topping knowledge. For the loftiest hill
That to the stars uncrowns his majesty,
Planting his stedfast footsteps in the sea,
Making the Heaven of Heavens his dwelling-place,
Spares but the cloudy border of his base
To the foil'd searching of mortality:
And thou, who didst the stars and sunbeams know,
Self-school'd, self-scann'd, self-honour'd, self-secure,
Didst walk on Earth unguess'd at. Better so!
All pains the immortal spirit must endure,
All weakness that impairs, all griefs that bow,
Find their sole voice in that victorious brow.

Resignation

TO FAUSTA

"To die be given us, or attain!
Fierce work it were, to do again."

So pilgrims, bound for Mecca, pray'd
At burning noon: so warriors said,
Scarf'd with the cross, who watch'd the miles
Of dust that wreath'd their struggling files
Down Lydian mountains: so, when snows
Round Alpine summits eddying rose,
The Goth, bound Rome-wards: so the Hun,
Crouch'd on his saddle, when the sun
Went lurid down o'er flooded plains
Through which the groaning Danube strains
To the drear Euxine: so pray all,
Whom labours, self-ordain'd, enthrall;
Because they to themselves propose
On this side the all-common close
A goal which, gain'd, may give repose.
So pray they: and to stand again
Where they stood once, to them were pain;
Pain to thread back and to renew
Past straits, and currents long steer'd through.

But milder natures, and more free;
Whom an unblam'd serenity
Hath freed from passions, and the state
Of struggle these necessitate;
Whom schooling of the stubborn mind
Hath made, or birth hath found, resign'd;
These mourn not, that their goings pay
Obedience to the passing day.
These claim not every laughing Hour
For handmaid to their striding power;
Each in her turn, with torch uprear'd,
To await their march; and when appear'd,
Through the cold gloom, with measur'd race,
To usher for a destin'd space,
(Her own sweet errands all foregone)
The too imperious Traveller on.
These, Fausta, ask not this: nor thou,
Time's chafing prisoner, ask it now.

We left, just ten years since, you say,
That wayside inn we left to-day:
Our jovial host, as forth we fare,

Shouts greeting from his easy chair;
High on a bank our leader stands,
Reviews and ranks his motley bands;
Makes clear our goal to every eye,
The valley's western boundary.
A gate swings to: our tide hath flow'd
Already from the silent road.
The valley pastures, one by one,
Are threaded, quiet in the sun:
And now beyond the rude stone bridge
Slopes gracious up the western ridge.
Its woody border, and the last
Of its dark upland farms is past:
Cool farms, with open-lying stores,
Under their burnish'd sycamores.
All past: and through the trees we glide
Emerging on the green hill-side.
There climbing hangs, a far-seen sign,
Our wavering, many-colour'd line;
There winds, upstreaming slowly still
Over the summit of the hill.
And now, in front, behold outspread
Those upper regions we must tread;
Mild hollows, and clear heathy swells,
The cheerful silence of the fells.
Some two hours' march, with serious air,
Through the deep noontide heats we fare:
The red-grouse, springing at our sound,
Skims, now and then, the shining ground;
No life, save his and ours, intrudes
Upon these breathless solitudes.
O joy! again the farms appear;
Cool shade is there, and rustic cheer:
There springs the brook will guide us down,
Bright comrade, to the noisy town.
Lingering, we follow down: we gain
The town, the highway, and the plain.
And many a mile of dusty way,
Parch'd and road-worn, we made that day;
But, Fausta, I remember well
That, as the balmy darkness fell,

We bath'd our hands, with speechless glee,
That night, in the wide-glimmering Sea.

Once more we tread this self-same road,
Fausta, which ten years since we trod:
Alone we tread it, you and I;
Ghosts of that boisterous company.
Here, where the brook shines, near its head,
In its clear, shallow, turf-fring'd bed;
Here, whence the eye first sees, far down,
Capp'd with faint smoke, the noisy town;
Here sit we, and again unroll,
Though slowly, the familiar whole.
The solemn wastes of heathy hill
Sleep in the July sunshine still:
The self-same shadows now, as then,
Play through this grassy upland glen:
The loose dark stones on the green way
Lie strewn, it seems, where then they lay:
On this mild bank above the stream,
(You crush them) the blue gentians gleam.
Still this wild brook, the rushes cool,
The sailing foam, the shining pool. —
These are not chang'd: and we, you say,
Are scarce more chang'd, in truth, than they.

The Gipsies, whom we met below,
They too have long roam'd to and fro.
They ramble, leaving, where they pass,
Their fragments on the cumber'd grass.
And often to some kindly place,
Chance guides the migratory race
Where, though long wanderings intervene,
They recognize a former scene.
The dingy tents are pitch'd: the fires
Give to the wind their wavering spires;
In dark knots crouch round the wild flame
Their children, as when first they came;
They see their shackled beasts again
Move, browsing, up the grey-wall'd lane.
Signs are not wanting, which might raise
The ghosts in them of former days:

Signs are not wanting, if they would;
Suggestions to disquietude.
For them, for all, Time's busy touch,
While it mends little, troubles much:
Their joints grow stiffer; but the year
Runs his old round of dubious cheer:
Chilly they grow; yet winds in March,
Still, sharp as ever, freeze and parch:
They must live still; and yet, God knows,
Crowded and keen the country grows:
It seems as if, in their decay,
The Law grew stronger every day.
So might they reason; so compare,
Fausta, times past with times that are.
But no: — they rubb'd through yesterday
In their hereditary way;
And they will rub through, if they can,
To-morrow on the self-same plan;
Till death arrives to supersede,
For them, vicissitude and need.

   The Poet, to whose mighty heart
Heaven doth a quicker pulse impart,
Subdues that energy to scan
Not his own course, but that of Man.
Though he move mountains; though his day
Be pass'd on the proud heights of sway;
Though he hath loos'd a thousand chains;
Though he hath borne immortal pains;
Action and suffering though he know;
— He hath not liv'd, if he lives so.
He sees, in some great-historied land,
A ruler of the people stand;
Sees his strong thought in fiery flood
Roll through the heaving multitude;
Exults: yet for no moment's space
Envies the all-regarded place.
Beautiful eyes meet his; and he
Bears to admire uncravingly:
They pass; he, mingled with the crowd,
Is in their far-off triumphs proud.

From some high station he looks down,
At sunset, on a populous town;
Surveys each happy group that fleets,
Toil ended, through the shining streets;
Each with some errand of its own; —
And does not say, "I am alone."
He sees the gentle stir of birth
When Morning purifies the earth;
He leans upon a gate, and sees
The pastures, and the quiet trees.
Low woody hill, with gracious bound,
Folds the still valley almost round;
The cuckoo, loud on some high lawn,
Is answer'd from the depth of dawn;
In the hedge straggling to the stream,
Pale, dew-drench'd, half-shut roses gleam:
But where the further side slopes down
He sees the drowsy new-wak'd clown
In his white quaint-embroider'd frock
Make, whistling, towards his mist-wreath'd flock;
Slowly, behind the heavy tread,
The wet flower'd grass heaves up its head. —
Lean'd on his gate, he gazes: tears
Are in his eyes, and in his ears
The murmur of a thousand years:
Before him he sees Life unroll,
A placid and continuous whole;
That general Life, which does not cease,
Whose secret is not joy, but peace;
That Life, whose dumb wish is not miss'd
If birth proceeds, if things subsist:
The Life of plants, and stones, and rain:
The Life he craves; if not in vain
Fate gave, what Chance shall not control,
His sad lucidity of soul.

You listen: — but that wandering smile,
Fausta, betrays you cold the while.
Your eyes pursue the bells of foam
Wash'd, eddying, from this bank, their home.
"Those Gipsies," so your thoughts I scan,

"Are less, the Poet more, than man.
They feel not, though they move and see:
Deeply the Poet feels; but he
Breathes, when he will, immortal air,
Where Orpheus and where Homer are.
In the day's life, whose iron round
Hems us all in, he is not bound.
He escapes thence, but we abide.
Not deep the Poet sees, but wide."

   The World in which we live and move
Outlasts aversion, outlasts love:
Outlasts each effort, interest, hope,
Remorse, grief, joy: — and were the scope
Of these affections wider made,
Man still would see, and see dismay'd,
Beyond his passion's widest range
Far regions of eternal change.
Nay, and since death, which wipes out man,
Finds him with many an unsolv'd plan,
With much unknown, and much untried,
Wonder not dead, and thirst not dried,
Still gazing on the ever full
Eternal mundane spectacle;
This World in which we draw our breath,
In some sense, Fausta, outlasts death.

   Blame thou not therefore him, who dares
Judge vain beforehand human cares.
Whose natural insight can discern
What through experience others learn.
Who needs not love and power, to know
Love transient, power an unreal show.
Who treads at ease life's uncheer'd ways: —
Him blame not, Fausta, rather praise.
Rather thyself for some aim pray
Nobler than this — to fill the day.
Rather, that heart, which burns in thee,
Ask, not to amuse, but to set free.
Be passionate hopes not ill resign'd
For quiet, and a fearless mind.
And though Fate grudge to thee and me

The Poet's rapt security,
Yet they, believe me, who await
No gifts from Chance, have conquer'd Fate.
They, winning room to see and hear,
And to men's business not too near,
Through clouds of individual strife
Draw homewards to the general Life.
Like leaves by suns not yet uncurl'd:
To the wise, foolish; to the world,
Weak: yet not weak, I might reply,
Not foolish, Fausta, in His eye,
To whom each moment in its race,
Crowd as we will its neutral space,
Is but a quiet watershed
Whence, equally, the Seas of Life and Death are fed.

　　Enough, we live: — and if a life,
With large results so little rife,
Though bearable, seem hardly worth
This pomp of worlds, this pain of birth;
Yet, Fausta, the mute turf we tread,
The solemn hills around us spread,
This stream that falls incessantly,
The strange-scrawl'd rocks, the lonely sky,
If I might lend their life a voice,
Seem to bear rather than rejoice.
And even could the intemperate prayer
Man iterates, while these forbear,
For movement, for an ampler sphere,
Pierce Fate's impenetrable ear;
Not milder is the general lot
Because our spirits have forgot,
In action's dizzying eddy whirl'd,
The something that infects the world.

To a Republican Friend, 1848

God knows it, I am with you. If to prize
Those virtues, priz'd and practis'd by too few,
But priz'd, but lov'd, but eminent in you,

Man's fundamental life: if to despise
The barren optimistic sophistries
Of comfortable moles, whom what they do
Teaches the limit of the just and true —
And for such doing have no need of eyes:
If sadness at the long heart-wasting show
Wherein earth's great ones are disquieted:
If thoughts, not idle, while before me flow
The armies of the homeless and unfed: —
   If these are yours, if this is what you are,
   Then am I yours, and what you feel, I share.

Memorial Verses

APRIL, 1850

Goethe in Weimar sleeps, and Greece,
Long since, saw Byron's struggle cease.
But one such death remain'd to come.
The last poetic voice is dumb.
What shall be said o'er Wordsworth's tomb?

When Byron's eyes were shut in death,
We bow'd our head and held our breath.
He taught us little: but our soul
Had *felt* him like the thunder's roll.
With shivering heart the strife we saw
Of Passion with Eternal Law.
And yet with reverential awe
We watch'd the fount of fiery life
Which serv'd for that Titanic strife.

When Goethe's death was told, we said —
Sunk, then, is Europe's sagest head.
Physician of the Iron Age
Goethe has done his pilgrimage.
He took the suffering human race,
He read each wound, each weakness clear —
And struck his finger on the place
And said — Thou ailest here, and here. —

He look'd on Europe's dying hour
Of fitful dream and feverish power;
His eye plung'd down the weltering strife,
The turmoil of expiring life;
He said — The end is everywhere:
Art still has truth, take refuge there. —
And he was happy, if to know
Causes of things, and far below
His feet to see the lurid flow
Of terror, and insane distress,
And headlong fate, be happiness.

And Wordsworth! — Ah, pale ghosts! rejoice!
For never has such soothing voice
Been to your shadowy world convey'd,
Since erst, at morn, some wandering shade
Heard the clear song of Orpheus come
Through Hades, and the mournful gloom.
Wordsworth is gone from us — and ye,
Ah, may ye feel his voice as we.
He too upon a wintry clime
Had fallen — on this iron time
Of doubts, disputes, distractions, fears.
He found us when the age had bound
Our souls in its benumbing round:
He spoke, and loos'd our heart in tears.
He laid us as we lay at birth
On the cool flowery lap of earth;
Smiles broke from us and we had ease.
The hills were round us, and the breeze
Went o'er the sun-lit fields again:
Our foreheads felt the wind and rain.
Our youth return'd: for there was shed
On spirits that had long been dead,
Spirits dried up and closely-furl'd,
The freshness of the early world.

Ah, since dark days still bring to light
Man's prudence and man's fiery might,
Time may restore us in his course
Goethe's sage mind and Byron's force:
But where will Europe's latter hour

Again find Wordsworth's healing power?
Others will teach us how to dare,
And against fear our breast to steel;
Others will strengthen us to bear —
But who, ah who, will make us feel?
The cloud of mortal destiny,
Others will front it fearlessly —
But who, like him, will put it by?
Keep fresh the grass upon his grave,
O Rotha! with thy living wave.
Sing him thy best! for few or none
Hears thy voice right, now he is gone.

The Buried Life

Light flows our war of mocking words, and yet,
Behold, with tears my eyes are wet.
I feel a nameless sadness o'er me roll.
Yes, yes, we know that we can jest,
We know, we know that we can smile;
But there's a something in this breast
To which thy light words bring no rest,
And thy gay smiles no anodyne.
Give me thy hand, and hush awhile,
And turn those limpid eyes on mine,
And let me read there, love, thy inmost soul.

Alas, is even Love too weak
To unlock the heart and let it speak?
Are even lovers powerless to reveal
To one another what indeed they feel?
I knew the mass of men conceal'd
Their thoughts, for fear that if reveal'd
They would by other men be met
With blank indifference, or with blame reprov'd:
I knew they liv'd and mov'd
Trick'd in disguises, alien to the rest
Of men, and alien to themselves — and yet
The same heart beats in every human breast.

But we, my love — does a like spell benumb
Our hearts — our voices? — must we too be dumb?

Ah, well for us, if even we,
Even for a moment, can get free
Our heart, and have our lips unchain'd:
For that which seals them hath been deep ordain'd.

Fate, which foresaw
How frivolous a baby man would be,
By what distractions he would be possess'd,
How he would pour himself in every strife,
And well-nigh change his own identity;
That it might keep from his capricious play
His genuine self, and force him to obey
Even in his own despite, his being's law,
Bade, through the deep recesses of our breast
The unregarded river of our life
Pursue with indiscernible flow its way;
And that we should not see
The buried stream, and seem to be
Eddying about in blind uncertainty,
Though driving on with it eternally.

But often in the world's most crowded streets,
But often, in the din of strife,
There rises an unspeakable desire
After the knowledge of our buried life,
A thirst to spend our fire and restless force
In tracking out our true, original course;
A longing to enquire
Into the mystery of this heart that beats
So wild, so deep in us, to know
Whence our thoughts come and where they go.
And many a man in his own breast then delves,
But deep enough, alas, none ever mines:
And we have been on many thousand lines,
And we have shown on each talent and power,
But hardly have we, for one little hour,
Been on our own line, have we been ourselves;
Hardly had skill to utter one of all
The nameless feelings that course through our breast,

But they course on for ever unexpress'd.
And long we try in vain to speak and act
Our hidden self, and what we say and do
Is eloquent, is well — but 'tis not true:
And then we will no more be rack'd
With inward striving, and demand
Of all the thousand nothings of the hour
Their stupefying power;
Ah yes, and they benumb us at our call:
Yet still, from time to time, vague and forlorn,
From the soul's subterranean depth upborne
As from an infinitely distant land,
Come airs, and floating echoes, and convey
A melancholy into all our day.

Only — but this is rare —
When a beloved hand is laid in ours,
When, jaded with the rush and glare
Of the interminable hours,
Our eyes can in another's eyes read clear,
When our world-deafen'd ear
Is by the tones of a loved voice caress'd,
A bolt is shot back somewhere in our breast
And a lost pulse of feeling stirs again:
The eye sinks inward, and the heart lies plain,
And what we mean, we say, and what we would, we know.
A man becomes aware of his life's flow
And hears its winding murmur, and he sees
The meadows where it glides, the sun, the breeze.

And there arrives a lull in the hot race
Wherein he doth for ever chase
That flying and elusive shadow, Rest.
An air of coolness plays upon his face,
And an unwonted calm pervades his breast.
And then he thinks he knows
The Hills where his life rose,
And the Sea where it goes.

Lines Written in Kensington Gardens

In this lone open glade I lie,
Screen'd by deep boughs on either hand;
And at its head, to stay the eye,
Those black-crown'd, red-boled pine-trees stand.

Birds here make song, each bird has his,
Across the girdling city's hum.
How green under the boughs it is!
How thick the tremulous sheep-cries come!

Sometimes a child will cross the glade
To take his nurse his broken toy;
Sometimes a thrush flit overhead
Deep in her unknown day's employ.

Here at my feet what wonders pass,
What endless active life is here!
What blowing daisies, fragrant grass!
An air-stirr'd forest, fresh and clear.

Scarce fresher is the mountain sod
Where the tired angler lies, stretch'd out,
And, eased of basket and of rod,
Counts his day's spoil, the spotted trout.

In the huge world which roars hard by
Be others happy, if they can!
But in my helpless cradle I
Was breathed on by the rural Pan.

I, on men's impious uproar hurl'd,
Think often, as I hear them rave,
That peace has left the upper world,
And now keeps only in the grave.

Yet here is peace for ever new!
When I, who watch them, am away,
Still all things in this glade go through
The changes of their quiet day.

Then to their happy rest they pass;
The flowers close, the birds are fed,

The night comes down upon the grass,
The child sleeps warmly in his bed.

Calm soul of all things! make it mine
To feel, amid the city's jar,
That there abides a peace of thine,
Man did not make, and cannot mar!

The will to neither strive nor cry,
The power to feel with others give!
Calm, calm me more! nor let me die
Before I have begun to live.

Indifference

I must not say that thou wert true,
Yet let me say that thou wert fair.
And they that lovely face who view,
They will not ask if truth be there.

Truth — what is truth? Two bleeding hearts
Wounded by men, by Fortune tried,
Outwearied with their lonely parts,
Vow to beat henceforth side by side.

The world to them was stern and drear;
Their lot was but to weep and moan.
Ah, let them keep their faith sincere,
For neither could subsist alone!

But souls whom some benignant breath
Has charm'd at birth from gloom and care,
These ask no love — these plight no faith,
For they are happy as they are.

The world to them may homage make,
And garlands for their forehead weave.
And what the world can give, they take:
But they bring more than they receive.

They smile upon the world: their ears
To one demand alone are coy.
They will not give us love and tears —
They bring us light, and warmth, and joy.

It was not love that heav'd thy breast,
Fair child! it was the bliss within.
Adieu! and say that one, at least,
Was just to what he did not win.

Absence

In this fair stranger's eyes of grey
Thine eyes, my love, I see.
I shudder: for the passing day
Had borne me far from thee.

This is the curse of life: that not
A nobler calmer train
Of wiser thoughts and feelings blot
Our passions from our brain;

But each day brings its petty dust
Our soon-chok'd souls to fill,
And we forget because we must,
And not because we will.

I struggle towards the light; and ye,
Once-long'd-for storms of love!
If with the light ye cannot be,
I bear that ye remove.

I struggle towards the light; but oh,
While yet the night is chill,
Upon Time's barren, stormy flow,
Stay with me, Marguerite, still!

A Summer Night

In the deserted moon-blanch'd street
How lonely rings the echo of my feet!
Those windows, which I gaze at, frown,
Silent and white, unopening down,
Repellent as the world: — but see!

A break between the housetops shows
The moon, and, lost behind her, fading dim
Into the dewy dark obscurity
Down at the far horizon's rim,
Doth a whole tract of heaven disclose.

And to my mind the thought
Is on a sudden brought
Of a past night, and a far different scene.
Headlands stood out into the moon-lit deep
As clearly as at noon;
The spring-tide's brimming flow
Heav'd dazzlingly between;
Houses with long white sweep
Girdled the glistening bay:
Behind, through the soft air,
The blue haze-cradled mountains spread away.
That night was far more fair;
But the same restless pacings to and fro
And the same vainly throbbing heart was there,
And the same bright calm moon.

And the calm moonlight seems to say —
— "Hast thou then still the old unquiet breast
That neither deadens into rest
Nor ever feels the fiery glow
That whirls the spirit from itself away,
But fluctuates to and fro
Never by passion quite possess'd,
And never quite benumb'd by the world's sway?" —
And I, I know not if to pray
Still to be what I am, or yield, and be
Like all the other men I see.

For most men in a brazen prison live,
Where in the sun's hot eye,
With heads bent o'er their toil, they languidly
Their lives to some unmeaning taskwork give,
Dreaming of nought beyond their prison wall:
And as, year after year,
Fresh products of their barren labour fall
From their tired hands, and rest

Never yet comes more near,
Gloom settles slowly down over their breast.
And while they try to stem
The waves of mournful thought by which they are prest,
Death in their prison reaches them
Unfreed, having seen nothing, still unblest.

And the rest, a few,
Escape their prison, and depart
On the wide Ocean of Life anew.
There the freed prisoner, where'er his heart
Listeth, will sail;
Nor does he know how there prevail,
Despotic on life's sea,
Trade-winds that cross it from eternity.
Awhile he holds some false sway, undebarr'd
By thwarting signs, and braves
The freshening wind and blackening waves.
And then the tempest strikes him, and between
The lightning bursts is seen
Only a driving wreck,
And the pale Master on his spar-strewn deck
With anguish'd face and flying hair
Grasping the rudder hard,
Still bent to make some port he knows not where,
Still standing for some false impossible shore.
And sterner comes the roar
Of sea and wind, and through the deepening gloom
Fainter and fainter wreck and helmsman loom,
And he too disappears, and comes no more.

Is there no life, but these alone?
Madman or slave, must man be one?

Plainness and clearness without shadow of stain,
Clearness divine!
Ye Heavens, whose pure dark regions have no sign
Of languor, though so calm, and though so great
Are yet untroubled and unpassionate:
Who, though so noble, share in the world's toil,
And though so task'd, keep free from dust and soil:
I will not say that your mild deeps retain

A tinge, it may be, of their silent pain
Who have long'd deeply once, and long'd in vain;
But I will rather say that you remain
A world above man's head, to let him see
How boundless might his soul's horizons be,
How vast, yet of what clear transparency.
How it were good to sink there, and breathe free.
How high a lot to fill
Is left to each man still.

Morality

We cannot kindle when we will
The fire that in the heart resides,
The spirit bloweth and is still,
In mystery our soul abides:
    But tasks in hours of insight will'd
    Can be through hours of gloom fulfill'd.

With aching hands and bleeding feet
We dig and heap, lay stone on stone;
We bear the burden and the heat
Of the long day, and wish 'twere done.
    Not till the hours of light return
    All we have built do we discern.

Then, when the clouds are off the soul,
When thou dost bask in Nature's eye,
Ask, how *she* view'd thy self-control,
Thy struggling task'd morality.
    Nature, whose free, light, cheerful air,
    Oft made thee, in thy gloom, despair.

And she, whose censure thou dost dread,
Whose eyes thou wert afraid to seek,
See, on her face a glow is spread,
A strong emotion on her cheek.
    "Ah child," she cries, "that strife divine—
    Whence was it, for it is not mine?

"There is no effort on *my* brow—
I do not strive, I do not weep.

I rush with the swift spheres, and glow
In joy, and, when I will, I sleep. —
  Yet that severe, that earnest air,
  I saw, I felt it once — but where?

"I knew not yet the gauge of Time,
Nor wore the manacles of Space.
I felt it in some other clime —
I saw it in some other place.
  — 'Twas when the heavenly house I trod,
  And lay upon the breast of God."

Stanzas in Memory of the Author of "Obermann"

In front the awful Alpine track
Crawls up its rocky stair;
The autumn storm-winds drive the rack
Close o'er it, in the air.

Behind are the abandoned baths
Mute in their meadows lone;
The leaves are on the valley paths;
The mists are on the Rhone —

The white mists rolling like a sea.
I hear the torrents roar.
  — Yes, Obermann, all speaks of thee!
I feel thee near once more.

I turn thy leaves: I feel their breath
Once more upon me roll;
That air of languor, cold, and death,
Which brooded o'er thy soul.

Fly hence, poor Wretch, whoe'er thou art,
Condemn'd to cast about,
All shipwreck in thy own weak heart,
For comfort from without:

A fever in these pages burns
Beneath the calm they feign;
A wounded human spirit turns
Here, on its bed of pain.

Yes, though the virgin mountain air
Fresh through these pages blows,
Though to these leaves the glaciers spare
The soul of their white snows,

Though here a mountain murmur swells
Of many a dark-bough'd pine,
Though, as you read, you hear the bells
Of the high-pasturing kine —

Yet, through the hum of torrent lone,
And brooding mountain bee,
There sobs I know not what ground tone
Of human agony.

Is it for this, because the sound
Is fraught too deep with pain,
That, Obermann! the world around
So little loves thy strain?

Some secrets may the poet tell,
For the world loves new ways.
To tell too deep ones is not well;
It knows not what he says.

Yet of the spirits who have reign'd
In this our troubled day,
I know but two, who have attain'd,
Save thee, to see their way.

By England's lakes, in grey old age,
His quiet home one keeps;
And one, the strong much-toiling Sage,
In German Weimar sleeps.

But Wordsworth's eyes avert their ken
From half of human fate;
And Goethe's course few sons of men
May think to emulate.

For he pursued a lonely road,
His eye on nature's plan;
Neither made man too much a God,
Nor God too much a man.

Strong was he, with a spirit free
From mists, and sane, and clear;

Clearer, how much! than ours: yet we
Have a worse course to steer.

For though his manhood bore the blast
Of a tremendous time,
Yet in a tranquil world was pass'd
His tenderer youthful prime.

But we, brought forth and rear'd in hours
Of change, alarm, surprise —
What shelter to grow ripe is ours?
What leisure to grow wise?

Like children bathing on the shore,
Buried a wave beneath,
The second wave succeeds, before
We have had time to breathe.

Too fast we live, too much are tried,
Too harass'd, to attain
Wordsworth's sweet calm, or Goethe's wide
And luminous view to gain.

And then we turn, thou sadder sage!
To thee: we feel thy spell.
The hopeless tangle of our age —
Thou too hast scann'd it well.

Immovable thou sittest; still
As death; compos'd to bear.
Thy head is clear, thy feeling chill —
And icy thy despair.

Yes, as the Son of Thetis said,
One hears thee saying now —
"Greater by far than thou are dead:
Strive not: die also thou." —

Ah! Two desires toss about
The poet's feverish blood.
One drives him to the world without,
And one to solitude.

"The glow," he cries, "the thrill of life —
Where, where do these abound?"

Not in the world, not in the strife
Of men, shall they be found.

He who hath watch'd, not shar'd, the strife,
Knows how the day hath gone;
He only lives with the world's life
Who hath renounc'd his own.

To thee we come, then. Clouds are roll'd
Where thou, O Seer, art set;
Thy realm of thought is drear and cold—
The world is colder yet!

And thou hast pleasures too to share
With those who come to thee:
Balms floating on thy mountain air,
And healing sights to see.

How often, where the slopes are green
On Jaman, hast thou sate
By some high chalet door, and seen
The summer day grow late,

And darkness steal o'er the wet grass
With the pale crocus starr'd,
And reach that glimmering sheet of glass
Beneath the piny sward,

Lake Leman's waters, far below:
And watch'd the rosy light
Fade from the distant peaks of snow:
And on the air of night

Heard accents of the eternal tongue
Through the pine branches play:
Listen'd, and felt thyself grow young;
Listen'd, and wept——Away!

Away the dreams that but deceive!
And thou, sad Guide, adieu!
I go; Fate drives me: but I leave
Half of my life with you.

We, in some unknown Power's employ,
Move on a rigorous line:

Can neither, when we will, enjoy;
Nor, when we will, resign.

I in the world must live: — but thou,
Thou melancholy Shade!
Wilt not, if thou can'st see me now,
Condemn me, nor upbraid.

For thou art gone away from earth,
And place with those dost claim,
The Children of the Second Birth
Whom the world could not tame;

And with that small transfigur'd Band,
Whom many a different way
Conducted to their common land,
Thou learn'st to think as they.

Christian and pagan, king and slave,
Soldier and anchorite,
Distinctions we esteem so grave,
Are nothing in their sight.

They do not ask, who pin'd unseen,
Who was on action hurl'd,
Whose one bond is that all have been
Unspotted by the world.

There without anger thou wilt see
Him who obeys thy spell
No more, so he but rest, like thee,
Unsoil'd: — and so, Farewell!

Farewell! — Whether thou now liest near
That much-lov'd inland sea,
The ripples of whose blue waves cheer
Vevey and Meillerie,

And in that gracious region bland,
Where with clear-rustling wave
The scented pines of Switzerland
Stand dark round thy green grave,

Between the dusty vineyard walls
Issuing on that green place

The early peasant still recalls
The pensive stranger's face,

And stoops to clear thy moss-grown date
Ere he plods on again; —
Or whether, by maligner Fate,
Among the swarms of men,

Where between granite terraces
The blue Seine rolls her wave,
The Capital of Pleasure sees
Thy hardly-heard-of grave —

Farewell! Under the sky we part,
In this stern Alpine dell.
O unstrung will! O broken heart!
A last, a last farewell!

The Future

A wanderer is man from his birth.
He was born in a ship
On the breast of the River of Time.
Brimming with wonder and joy
He spreads out his arms to the light,
Rivets his gaze on the banks of the stream.

As what he sees is, so have his thoughts been.
Whether he wakes
Where the snowy mountainous pass
Echoing the screams of the eagles
Hems in its gorges the bed
Of the new-born clear-flowing stream:

Whether he first sees light
Where the river in gleaming rings
Sluggishly winds through the plain:
Whether in sound of the swallowing sea: —
As is the world on the banks
So is the mind of the man.

Vainly does each as he glides
Fable and dream

Of the lands which the River of Time
Had left ere he woke on its breast,
Or shall reach when his eyes have been clos'd.
Only the tract where he sails
He wots of: only the thoughts,
Rais'd by the objects he passes, are his.

Who can see the green Earth any more
As she was by the sources of Time?
Who imagines her fields as they lay
In the sunshine, unworn by the plough?
Who thinks as they thought,
The tribes who then roam'd on her breast,
Her vigorous primitive sons?

What girl
Now reads in her bosom as clear
As Rebekah read, when she sate
At eve by the palm-shaded well?
Who guards in her breast
As deep, as pellucid a spring
Of feeling, as tranquil, as sure?

What Bard,
At the height of his vision, can deem
Of God, of the world, of the soul,
With a plainness as near,
As flashing as Moses felt,
When he lay in the night by his flock
On the starlit Arabian waste?
Can rise and obey
The beck of the Spirit like him?

This tract which the River of Time
Now flows through with us, is the Plain.
Gone is the calm of its earlier shore.
Border'd by cities and hoarse
With a thousand cries is its stream.
And we on its breast, our minds
Are confus'd as the cries which we hear,
Changing and shot as the sights which we see.

And we say that repose has fled
For ever the course of the River of Time.

That cities will crowd to its edge
In a blacker incessanter line;
That the din will be more on its banks,
Denser the trade on its stream,
Flatter the plain where it flows,
Fiercer the sun overhead.
That never will those on its breast
See an ennobling sight,
Drink of the feeling of quiet again.

But what was before us we know not,
And we know not what shall succeed.

Haply, the River of Time,
As it grows, as the towns on its marge
Fling their wavering lights
On a wider statelier stream —
May acquire, if not the calm
Of its early mountainous shore,
Yet a solemn peace of its own.

And the width of the waters, the hush
Of the grey expanse where he floats,
Freshening its current and spotted with foam
As it draws to the Ocean, may strike
Peace to the soul of the man on its breast:
As the pale waste widens around him —
As the banks fade dimmer away —
As the stars come out, and the night-wind
Brings up the stream
Murmurs and scents of the infinite Sea.

The Scholar Gipsy

"There was very lately a lad in the University of Oxford who was by
his poverty forced to leave his studies there; and at last to join himself
to a company of vagabond gipsies. Among these extravagant people, by
the insinuating subtilty of his carriage, he quickly got so much of their
love and esteem as that they discovered to him their mystery. After he

had been a pretty while well exercised in the trade, there chanced to ride by a couple of scholars, who had formerly been of his acquaintance. They quickly spied out their old friend among the gipsies; and he gave them an account of the necessity which drove him to that kind of life, and told them that the people he went with were not such impostors as they were taken for, but that they had a traditional kind of learning among them, and could do wonders by the power of imagination, their fancy binding that of others: that himself had learned much of their art, and when he had compassed the whole secret, he intended, he said, to leave their company, and give the world an account of what he had learned." — GLANVIL'S *Vanity of Dogmatizing*, 1661.

Go, for they call you, Shepherd, from the hill;
   Go, Shepherd, and untie the wattled cotes:
      No longer leave thy wistful flock unfed,
   Nor let thy bawling fellows rack their throats,
      Nor the cropp'd grasses shoot another head.
         But when the fields are still,
   And the tired men and dogs all gone to rest,
      And only the white sheep are sometimes seen
      Cross and recross the strips of moon-blanch'd green;
         Come, Shepherd, and again renew the quest.

Here, where the reaper was at work of late,
   In this high field's dark corner, where he leaves
      His coat, his basket, and his earthen cruise,
   And in the sun all morning binds the sheaves,
      Then here, at noon, comes back his stores to use;
         Here will I sit and wait,
   While to my ear from uplands far away
      The bleating of the folded flocks is borne,
      With distant cries of reapers in the corn —
         All the live murmur of a summer's day.

Screen'd is this nook o'er the high, half-reap'd field,
   And here till sun-down, Shepherd, will I be.
      Through the thick corn the scarlet poppies peep
   And round green roots and yellowing stalks I see
      Pale blue convolvulus in tendrils creep:
         And air-swept lindens yield

Their scent, and rustle down their perfum'd showers
   Of bloom on the bent grass where I am laid,
    And bower me from the August sun with shade;
      And the eye travels down to Oxford's towers:

And near me on the grass lies Glanvil's book—
   Come, let me read the oft-read tale again,
    The story of that Oxford scholar poor
Of pregnant parts and quick inventive brain,
    Who, tir'd of knocking at Preferment's door,
      One summer morn forsook
His friends, and went to learn the Gipsy lore,
    And roam'd the world with that wild brotherhood,
    And came, as most men deem'd, to little good,
      But came to Oxford and his friends no more.

But once, years after, in the country lanes,
   Two scholars whom at college erst he knew
    Met him, and of his way of life enquir'd.
Whereat he answer'd, that the Gipsy crew,
    His mates, had arts to rule as they desir'd
      The workings of men's brains;
And they can bind them to what thoughts they will:
    "And I," he said, "the secret of their art,
    When fully learn'd, will to the world impart:
      But it needs heaven-sent moments for this skill."

This said, he left them, and return'd no more,
   But rumours hung about the country side
    That the lost Scholar long was seen to stray,
Seen by rare glimpses, pensive and tongue-tied,
    In hat of antique shape, and cloak of grey,
      The same the Gipsies wore.
Shepherds had met him on the Hurst in spring:
    At some lone alehouse in the Berkshire moors,
    On the warm ingle bench, the smock-frock'd boors
      Had found him seated at their entering,

But, mid their drink and clatter, he would fly:
   And I myself seem half to know thy looks,
    And put the shepherds, Wanderer, on thy trace;
And boys who in lone wheatfields scare the rooks
    I ask if thou hast pass'd their quiet place;

Or in my boat I lie
Moor'd to the cool bank in the summer heats,
    Mid wide grass meadows which the sunshine fills,
    And watch the warm green-muffled Cumner hills,
        And wonder if thou haunt'st their shy retreats.

For most, I know, thou lov'st retired ground.
    Thee, at the ferry, Oxford riders blithe,
        Returning home on summer nights, have met
    Crossing the stripling Thames at Bab-lock-hithe,
        Trailing in the cool stream thy fingers wet,
            As the slow punt swings round:
    And leaning backwards in a pensive dream,
        And fostering in thy lap a heap of flowers
        Pluck'd in shy fields and distant Wychwood bowers,
            And thine eyes resting on the moonlit stream.

And then they land, and thou art seen no more.
    Maidens who from the distant hamlets come
        To dance around the Fyfield elm in May,
    Oft through the darkening fields have seen thee roam,
        Or cross a stile into the public way.
            Oft thou hast given them store
    Of flowers — the frail-leaf'd, white anemone —
        Dark bluebells drench'd with dews of summer eves —
        And purple orchises with spotted leaves —
            But none has words she can report of thee.

And, above Godstow Bridge, when hay-time's here
    In June, and many a scythe in sunshine flames,
        Men who through those wide fields of breezy grass
    Where black-wing'd swallows haunt the glittering Thames,
        To bathe in the abandon'd lasher pass,
            Have often pass'd thee near
    Sitting upon the river bank o'ergrown:
        Mark'd thy outlandish garb, thy figure spare,
        Thy dark vague eyes, and soft abstracted air;
            But, when they came from bathing, thou wert gone.

At some lone homestead in the Cumner hills,
    Where at her open door the housewife darns,
        Thou hast been seen, or hanging on a gate
    To watch the threshers in the mossy barns.

Children, who early range these slopes and late
   For cresses from the rills,
Have known thee watching, all an April day,
   The springing pastures and the feeding kine;
   And mark'd thee, when the stars come out and shine,
     Through the long dewy grass move slow away.

In Autumn, on the skirts of Bagley wood,
   Where most the Gipsies by the turf-edg'd way
    Pitch their smok'd tents, and every bush you see
With scarlet patches tagg'd and shreds of grey,
   Above the forest ground call'd Thessaly —
    The blackbird picking food
Sees thee, nor stops his meal, nor fears at all;
   So often has he known thee past him stray
   Rapt, twirling in thy hand a wither'd spray,
    And waiting for the spark from Heaven to fall.

And once, in winter, on the causeway chill
   Where home through flooded fields foot-travellers go,
    Have I not pass'd thee on the wooden bridge
Wrapt in thy cloak and battling with the snow,
   Thy face towards Hinksey and its wintry ridge?
    And thou hast climb'd the hill
And gain'd the white brow of the Cumner range,
   Turn'd once to watch, while thick the snowflakes fall,
   The line of festal light in Christ-Church hall —
    Then sought thy straw in some sequester'd grange.

But what — I dream! Two hundred years are flown
   Since first thy story ran through Oxford halls,
    And the grave Glanvil did the tale inscribe
That thou wert wander'd from the studious walls
   To learn strange arts, and join a Gipsy tribe:
    And thou from earth art gone
Long since, and in some quiet churchyard laid;
   Some country nook, where o'er thy unknown grave
   Tall grasses and white flowering nettles wave —
    Under a dark red-fruited yew-tree's shade.

— No, no, thou hast not felt the lapse of hours.
   For what wears out the life of mortal men?
    'Tis that from change to change their being rolls:

'Tis that repeated shocks, again, again,
    Exhaust the energy of strongest souls,
        And numb the elastic powers.
Till having us'd our nerves with bliss and teen,
    And tir'd upon a thousand schemes our wit,
        To the just-pausing Genius we remit
        Our worn-out life, and are — what we have been.

Thou hast not liv'd, why should'st thou perish, so?
    Thou hadst *one* aim, *one* business, *one* desire:
        Else wert thou long since number'd with the dead —
Else hadst thou spent, like other men, thy fire.
    The generations of thy peers are fled,
        And we ourselves shall go;
But thou possessest an immortal lot,
    And we imagine thee exempt from age
    And living as thou liv'st on Glanvil's page,
        Because thou hadst — what we, alas, have not!

For early didst thou leave the world, with powers
    Fresh, undiverted to the world without,
        Firm to their mark, not spent on other things;
Free from the sick fatigue, the languid doubt,
    Which much to have tried, in much been baffled, brings.
        O Life unlike to ours!
Who fluctuate idly without term or scope,
    Of whom each strives, nor knows for what he strives,
    And each half lives a hundred different lives;
        Who wait like thee, but not, like thee, in hope.

Thou waitest for the spark from Heaven: and we,
    Light half-believers of our casual creeds,
    Who never deeply felt, nor clearly will'd,
Whose insight never has borne fruit in deeds,
    Whose vague resolves never have been fulfill'd;
        For whom each year we see
Breeds new beginnings, disappointments new;
    Who hesitate and falter life away,
    And lose to-morrow the ground won to-day —
        Ah, do not we, Wanderer, await it too?

Yes, we await it, but it still delays,
    And then we suffer; and amongst us One,

Who most has suffer'd, takes dejectedly
His seat upon the intellectual throne;
    And all his store of sad experience he
        Lays bare of wretched days;
Tells us his misery's birth and growth and signs,
    And how the dying spark of hope was fed,
    And how the breast was sooth'd, and how the head,
        And all his hourly varied anodynes.

This for our wisest: and we others pine,
    And wish the long unhappy dream would end,
        And waive all claim to bliss, and try to bear
With close-lipp'd Patience for our only friend,
        Sad Patience, too near neighbour to Despair:
            But none has hope like thine.
Thou through the fields and through the woods dost stray,
    Roaming the country side, a truant boy,
    Nursing thy project in unclouded joy,
        And every doubt long blown by time away.

O born in days when wits were fresh and clear,
    And life ran gaily as the sparkling Thames;
        Before this strange disease of modern life,
With its sick hurry, its divided aims,
        Its heads o'ertax'd, its palsied hearts, was rife —
            Fly hence, our contact fear!
Still fly, plunge deeper in the bowering wood!
    Averse, as Dido did with gesture stern
    From her false friend's approach in Hades turn,
        Wave us away, and keep thy solitude.

Still nursing the unconquerable hope,
    Still clutching the inviolable shade,
        With a free onward impulse brushing through,
By night, the silver'd branches of the glade —
        Far on the forest skirts, where none pursue
            On some mild pastoral slope
Emerge, and resting on the moonlit pales,
    Freshen thy flowers, as in former years,
    With dew, or listen with enchanted ears,
        From the dark dingles, to the nightingales.

But fly our paths, our feverish contact fly!
   For strong the infection of our mental strife,
      Which, though it gives no bliss, yet spoils for rest;
   And we should win thee from thy own fair life,
     Like us distracted, and like us unblest.
        Soon, soon thy cheer would die,
   Thy hopes grow timorous, and unfix'd thy powers,
     And thy clear aims be cross and shifting made:
   And then thy glad perennial youth would fade,
      Fade, and grow old at last, and die like ours.

Then fly our greetings, fly our speech and smiles!
   —As some grave Tyrian trader, from the sea,
     Descried at sunrise an emerging prow
   Lifting the cool-hair'd creepers stealthily,
     The fringes of a southward-facing brow
       Among the Aegean isles:
   And saw the merry Grecian coaster come,
     Freighted with amber grapes, and Chian wine,
     Green bursting figs, and tunnies steep'd in brine;
     And knew the intruders on his ancient home,

The young light-hearted Masters of the waves;
   And snatch'd his rudder, and shook out more sail,
     And day and night held on indignantly
   O'er the blue Midland waters with the gale,
     Betwixt the Syrtes and soft Sicily,
       To where the Atlantic raves
   Outside the Western Straits, and unbent sails
     There, where down cloudy cliffs, through sheets of foam,
     Shy traffickers, the dark Iberians come;
     And on the beach undid his corded bales.

Sohrab and Rustum

An Episode

And the first grey of morning fill'd the east,
And the fog rose out of the Oxus stream.
But all the Tartar camp along the stream

Was hush'd, and still the men were plunged in sleep:
Sohrab alone, he slept not: all night long
He had lain wakeful, tossing on his bed;
But when the grey dawn stole into his tent,
He rose, and clad himself, and girt his sword,
And took his horseman's cloak, and left his tent,
And went abroad into the cold wet fog,
Through the dim camp to Peran-Wisa's tent.
    Through the black Tartar tents he pass'd, which stood
Clustering like bee-hives on the low flat strand
Of Oxus, where the summer floods o'erflow
When the sun melts the snows in high Pamere:
Through the black tents he pass'd, o'er that low strand,
And to a hillock came, a little back
From the stream's brink, the spot where first a boat,
Crossing the stream in summer, scrapes the land.
The men of former times had crown'd the top
With a clay fort: but that was fall'n; and now
The Tartars built there Peran-Wisa's tent,
A dome of laths, and o'er it felts were spread.
And Sohrab came there, and went in, and stood
Upon the thick-pil'd carpets in the tent,
And found the old man sleeping on his bed
Of rugs and felts, and near him lay his arms.
And Peran-Wisa heard him, though the step
Was dull'd; for he slept light, an old man's sleep;
And he rose quickly on one arm, and said: —
    "Who art thou? for it is not yet clear dawn.
Speak! is there news, or any night alarm?"
    But Sohrab came to the bedside, and said: —
"Thou know'st me, Peran-Wisa: it is I.
The sun is not yet risen, and the foe
Sleep; but I sleep not; all night long I lie
Tossing and wakeful, and I come to thee.
For so did King Afrasiab bid me seek
Thy counsel, and to heed thee as thy son,
In Samarcand, before the army march'd;
And I will tell thee what my heart desires.
Thou knowest if, since from Ader-baijan first
I came among the Tartars, and bore arms,
I have still serv'd Afrasiab well, and shown,

At my boy's years, the courage of a man.
This too thou know'st, that, while I still bear on
The conquering Tartar ensigns through the world,
And beat the Persians back on every field,
I seek one man, one man, and one alone —
Rustum, my father; who, I·hop'd, should greet,
Should one day greet, upon some well-fought field
His not unworthy, not inglorious son.
So I long hop'd, but him I never find.
Come then, hear now, and grant me what I ask.
Let the two armies rest to-day: but I
Will challenge forth the bravest Persian lords
To meet me, man to man: if I prevail,
Rustum will surely hear it; if I fall —
Old man, the dead need no one, claim no kin.
Dim is the rumour of a common fight,
Where host meets host, and many names are sunk:
But of a single combat Fame speaks clear."
　　He spoke: and Peran-Wisa took the hand
Of the young man in his, and sigh'd, and said: —
　　"O Sohrab, an unquiet heart is thine!
Canst thou not rest among the Tartar chiefs,
And share the battle's common chance with us
Who love thee, but must press for ever first,
In single fight incurring single risk,
To find a father thou hast never seen?
That were far best, my son, to stay with us
Unmurmuring; in our tents, while it is war,
And when 'tis truce, then in Afrasiab's towns.
But, if this one desire indeed rules all,
To seek out Rustum — seek him not through fight:
Seek him in peace, and carry to his arms,
O Sohrab, carry an unwounded son!
But far hence seek him, for he is not here.
For now it is not as when I was young,
When Rustum was in front of every fray:
But now he keeps apart, and sits at home,
In Seistan, with Zal, his father old.
Whether that his own mighty strength at last
Feels the abhorr'd approaches of old age;
Or in some quarrel with the Persian King.

There go: — Thou wilt not? Yet my heart forebodes
Danger or death awaits thee on this field.
Fain would I know thee safe and well, though lost
To us: fain therefore send thee hence, in peace
To seek thy father, not seek single fights
In vain: — but who can keep the lion's cub
From ravening? and who govern Rustum's son?
Go: I will grant thee what thy heart desires."
    So said he, and dropp'd Sohrab's hand, and left
His bed, and the warm rugs whereon he lay,
And o'er his chilly limbs his woollen coat
He pass'd, and tied his sandals on his feet,
And threw a white cloak round him, and he took
In his right hand a ruler's staff, no sword;
And on his head he placed his sheep-skin cap,
Black, glossy, curl'd, the fleece of Kara-Kul;
And rais'd the curtain of his tent, and call'd
His herald to his side, and went abroad.
    The sun, by this, had risen, and clear'd the fog
From the broad Oxus and the glittering sands:
And from their tents the Tartar horsemen fil'd
Into the open plain; so Haman bade;
Haman, who next to Peran-Wisa rul'd
The host, and still was in his lusty prime.
From their black tents, long files of horse, they stream'd:
As when, some grey November morn, the files,
In marching order spread, of long-neck'd cranes
Stream over Casbin, and the southern slopes
Of Elburz, from the Aralian estuaries,
Or some frore Caspian reed-bed, southward bound
For the warm Persian sea-board: so they stream'd.
The Tartars of the Oxus, the King's guard,
First with black sheep-skin caps and with long spears;
Large men, large steeds; who from Bokhara come
And Khiva, and ferment the milk of mares.
Next the more temperate Toorkmuns of the south,
The Tukas, and the lances of Salore,
And those from Attruck and the Caspian sands;
Light men, and on light steeds, who only drink
The acrid milk of camels, and their wells.
And then a swarm of wandering horse, who came

From far, and a more doubtful service own'd;
The Tartars of Ferghana, from the banks'
Of the Jaxartes, men with scanty beards
And close-set skull-caps; and those wilder hordes
Who roam o'er Kipchak and the northern waste
Kalmuks and unkemp'd Kuzzaks, tribes who stray
Nearest the Pole, and wandering Kirghizzes,
Who come on shaggy ponies from Pamere.
These all fil'd out from camp into the plain.
And on the other side the Persians form'd:
First a light cloud of horse, Tartars they seem'd,
The Ilyats of Khorassan: and behind,
The royal troops of Persia, horse and foot,
Marshall'd battalions bright in burnish'd steel.
But Peran-Wisa with his herald came
Threading the Tartar squadrons to the front,
And with his staff kept back the foremost ranks.
And when Ferood, who led the Persians, saw
That Peran-Wisa kept the Tartars back,
He took his spear, and to the front he came,
And check'd his ranks, and fix'd them where they stood.
And the old Tartar came upon the sand
Betwixt the silent hosts, and spake, and said: —
    "Ferood, and ye, Persians and Tartars, hear!
Let there be truce between the hosts to-day.
But choose a champion from the Persian lords
To fight our champion Sohrab, man to man."
    As, in the country, on a morn in June,
When the dew glistens on the pearled ears,
A shiver runs through the deep corn for joy —
So, when they heard what Peran-Wisa said,
A thrill through all the Tartar squadrons ran
Of pride and hope for Sohrab, whom they lov'd.
    But as a troop of pedlars, from Cabool,
Cross underneath the Indian Caucasus,
That vast sky-neighbouring mountain of milk snow;
Winding so high, that, as they mount, they pass
Long flocks of travelling birds dead on the snow,
Chok'd by the air, and scarce can they themselves
Slake their parch'd throats with sugar'd mulberries —
In single file they move, and stop their breath,

For fear they should dislodge the o'erhanging snows —
So the pale Persians held their breath with fear.
    And to Ferood his brother Chiefs came up
To counsel: Gudurz and Zoarrah came,
And Feraburz, who rul'd the Persian host
Second, and was the uncle of the King:
These came and counsell'd; and then Gudurz said:
    "Ferood, shame bids us take their challenge up,
Yet champion have we none to match this youth.
He has the wild stag's foot, the lion's heart.
But Rustum came last night; aloof he sits
And sullen, and has pitch'd his tents apart:
Him will I seek, and carry to his ear
The Tartar challenge, and this young man's name.
Haply he will forget his wrath, and fight.
Stand forth the while, and take their challenge up."
    So spake he; and Ferood stood forth and said: —
"Old man, be it agreed as thou hast said.
Let Sohrab arm, and we will find a man."
    He spoke; and Peran-Wisa turn'd, and strode
Back through the opening squadrons to his tent.
But through the anxious Persians Gudurz ran,
And cross'd the camp which lay behind, and reach'd,
Out on the sands beyond it, Rustum's tents.
Of scarlet cloth they were, and glittering gay,
Just pitch'd: the high pavilion in the midst
Was Rustum's, and his men lay camp'd around.
And Gudurz enter'd Rustum's tent, and found
Rustum: his morning meal was done, but still
The table stood beside him, charg'd with food;
A side of roasted sheep, and cakes of bread,
And dark green melons; and there Rustum sate
Listless, and held a falcon on his wrist,
And play'd with it; but Gudurz came and stood
Before him; and he look'd, and saw him stand;
And with a cry sprang up, and dropp'd the bird,
And greeted Gudurz with both hands, and said: —
    "Welcome! these eyes could see no better sight.
What news? but sit down first, and eat and drink."
    But Gudurz stood in the tent door, and said: —
"Not now: a time will come to eat and drink,

But not to-day: to-day has other needs.
The armies are drawn out, and stand at gaze:
For from the Tartars is a challenge brought
To pick a champion from the Persian lords
To fight their champion — and thou know'st his name —
Sohrab men call him, but his birth is hid.
O Rustum, like thy might is this young man's!
He has the wild stag's foot, the lion's heart.
And he is young, and Iran's Chiefs are old,
Or else too weak; and all eyes turn to thee.
Come down and help us, Rustum, or we lose."
    He spoke: but Rustum answer'd with a smile: —
"Go to! if Iran's Chiefs are old, then I
Am older: if the young are weak, the King
Errs strangely: for the King, for Kai Khosroo,
Himself is young, and honours younger men,
And lets the aged moulder to their graves.
Rustum he loves no more, but loves the young —
The young may rise at Sohrab's vaunts, not I.
For what care I, though all speak Sohrab's fame?
For would that I myself had such a son,
And not that one slight helpless girl I have,
A son so fam'd, so brave, to send to war,
And I to tarry with the snow-hair'd Zal,
My father, whom the robber Afghans vex,
And clip his borders short, and drive his herds,
And he has none to guard his weak old age.
There would I go, and hang my armour up,
And with my great name fence that weak old man,
And spend the goodly treasures I have got,
And rest my age, and hear of Sohrab's fame,
And leave to death the hosts of thankless kings,
And with these slaughterous hands draw sword no more."
    He spoke, and smil'd; and Gudurz made reply: —
"What then, O Rustum, will men say to this,
When Sohrab dares our bravest forth, and seeks
Thee most of all, and thou, whom most he seeks,
Hidest thy face? Take heed, lest men should say,
Like some old miser, Rustum hoards his fame,
And shuns to peril it with younger men."
    And, greatly mov'd, then Rustum made reply: —

"O Gudurz, wherefore dost thou say such words?
Thou knowest better words than this to say.
What is one more, one less, obscure or fam'd,
Valiant or craven, young or old, to me?
Are not they mortal, am not I myself?
But who for men of nought would do great deeds?
Come, thou shalt see how Rustum hoards his fame.
But I will fight unknown, and in plain arms;
Let not men say of Rustum, he was match'd
In single fight with any mortal man."

   He spoke, and frown'd; and Gudurz turn'd, and ran
Back quickly through the camp in fear and joy,
Fear at his wrath, but joy that Rustum came.
But Rustum strode to his tent door, and call'd
His followers in, and bade them bring his arms,
And clad himself in steel: the arms he chose
Were plain, and on his shield was no device,
Only his helm was rich, inlaid with gold,
And from the fluted spine atop a plume
Of horsehair wav'd, a scarlet horsehair plume.
So arm'd he issued forth; and Ruksh, his horse,
Follow'd him, like a faithful hound, at heel,
Ruksh, whose renown was nois'd through all the earth,
The horse, whom Rustum on a foray once
Did in Bokhara by the river find
A colt beneath its dam, and drove him home,
And rear'd him; a bright bay, with lofty crest;
Dight with a saddle-cloth of broider'd green
Crusted with gold, and on the ground were work'd
All beasts of chase, all beasts which hunters know:
So follow'd, Rustum left his tents, and cross'd
The camp, and to the Persian host appear'd.
And all the Persians knew him, and with shouts
Hail'd; but the Tartars knew not who he was.
And dear as the wet diver to the eyes
Of his pale wife who waits and weeps on shore,
By sandy Bahrein, in the Persian Gulf,
Plunging all day in the blue waves, at night,
Having made up his tale of precious pearls,
Rejoins her in their hut upon the sands —
So dear to the pale Persians Rustum came.

And Rustum to the Persian front advanc'd,
And Sohrab arm'd in Haman's tent, and came.
And as afield the reapers cut a swathe
Down through the middle of a rich man's corn,
And on each side are squares of standing corn,
And in the midst a stubble, short and bare;
So on each side were squares of men, with spears
Bristling, and in the midst, the open sand.
And Rustum came upon the sand, and cast
His eyes towards the Tartar tents, and saw
Sohrab come forth, and ey'd him as he came.
    As some rich woman, on a winter's morn,
Eyes through her silken curtains the poor drudge
Who with numb blacken'd fingers makes her fire —
At cock-crow, on a starlit winter's morn,
When the frost flowers the whiten'd window panes —
And wonders how she lives, and what the thoughts
Of that poor drudge may be; so Rustum ey'd
The unknown adventurous Youth, who from afar
Came seeking Rustum, and defying forth
All the most valiant chiefs: long he perus'd
His spirited air, and wonder'd who he was.
For very young he seem'd, tenderly rear'd;
Like some young cypress, tall, and dark, and straight,
Which in a queen's secluded garden throws
Its slight dark shadow on the moonlit turf,
By midnight, to a bubbling fountain's sound —
So slender Sohrab seem'd, so softly rear'd.
And a deep pity enter'd Rustum's soul
As he beheld him coming; and he stood,
And beckon'd to him with his hand, and said: —
    "O thou young man, the air of Heaven is soft,
And warm, and pleasant; but the grave is cold.
Heaven's air is better than the cold dead grave.
Behold me: I am vast, and clad in iron,
And tried; and I have stood on many a field
Of blood, and I have fought with many a foe:
Never was that field lost, or that foe sav'd.
O Sohrab, wherefore wilt thou rush on death?
Be govern'd: quit the Tartar host, and come
To Iran, and be as my son to me,

And fight beneath my banner till I die.
There are no youths in Iran brave as thou."
    So he spake, mildly: Sohrab heard his voice,
The mighty voice of Rustum; and he saw
His giant figure planted on the sand,
Sole, like some single tower, which a chief
Has builded on the waste in former years
Against the robbers; and he saw that head,
Streak'd with its first grey hairs: hope fill'd his soul;
And he ran forwards and embrac'd his knees,
And clasp'd his hand within his own and said: —
    "Oh, by thy father's head! by thine own soul!
Art thou not Rustum? Speak! art thou not he?"
    But Rustum ey'd askance the kneeling youth,
And turn'd away, and spoke to his own soul: —
    "Ah me, I muse what this young fox may mean.
False, wily, boastful, are these Tartar boys.
For if I now confess this thing he asks,
And hide it not, but say — *Rustum is here* —
He will not yield indeed, nor quit our foes,
But he will find some pretext not to fight,
And praise my fame, and proffer courteous gifts,
A belt or sword perhaps, and go his way.
And on a feast-tide, in Afrasiab's hall,
In Samarcand, he will arise and cry —
'I challeng'd once, when the two armies camp'd
Beside the Oxus, all the Persian lords
To cope with me in single fight; but they
Shrank; only Rustum dar'd: then he and I
Chang'd gifts, and went on equal terms away.'
So will he speak, perhaps, while men applaud.
Then were the chiefs of Iran sham'd through me."
    And then he turn'd, and sternly spake aloud: —
"Rise! wherefore dost thou vainly question thus
Of Rustum? I am here, whom thou hast call'd
By challenge forth: make good thy vaunt, or yield
Is it with Rustum only thou wouldst fight?
Rash boy, men look on Rustum's face and flee.
For well I know, that did great Rustum stand
Before thy face this day, and were reveal'd,
There would be then no talk of fighting more.

But being what I am, I tell thee this;
Do thou record it in thine inmost soul:
Either thou shalt renounce thy vaunt, and yield;
Or else thy bones shall strew this sand, till winds
Bleach them, or Oxus with his summer floods,
Oxus in summer wash them all away."
   He spoke: and Sohrab answer'd, on his feet: —
"Art thou so fierce? Thou wilt not fright me so.
I am no girl, to be made pale by words.
Yet this thou hast said well, did Rustum stand
Here on this field, there were no fighting then.
But Rustum is far hence, and we stand here.
Begin: thou art more vast, more dread than I,
And thou art prov'd, I know, and I am young —
But yet Success sways with the breath of Heaven.
And though thou thinkest that thou knowest sure
Thy victory, yet thou canst not surely know.
For we are all, like swimmers in the sea,
Pois'd on the top of a huge wave of Fate,
Which hangs uncertain to which side to fall.
And whether it will heave us up to land,
Or whether it will roll us out to sea,
Back out to sea, to the deep waves of death,
We know not, and no search will make us know:
Only the event will teach us in its hour."
   He spoke; and Rustum answer'd not, but hurl'd
His spear: down from the shoulder, down it came,
As on some partridge in the corn a hawk
That long has tower'd in the airy clouds
Drops like a plummet: Sohrab saw it come,
And sprang aside, quick as a flash: the spear
Hiss'd, and went quivering down into the sand,
Which it sent flying wide: — then Sohrab threw
In turn, and full struck Rustum's shield: sharp rang,
The iron plates rang sharp, but turn'd the spear.
And Rustum seiz'd his club, which none but he
Could wield: an unlopp'd trunk it was, and huge,
Still rough; like those which men in treeless plains
To build them boats fish from the flooded rivers,
Hyphasis or Hydaspes, when, high up
By their dark springs, the wind in winter-time

Has made in Himalayan forests wrack,
And strewn the channels with torn boughs; so huge
The club which Rustum lifted now, and struck
One stroke; but again Sohrab sprang aside
Lithe as the glancing snake, and the club came
Thundering to earth, and leapt from Rustum's hand.
And Rustum follow'd his own blow, and fell
To his knees, and with his fingers clutch'd the sand:
And now might Sohrab have unsheath'd his sword,
And pierc'd the mighty Rustum while he lay
Dizzy, and on his knees, and chok'd with sand:
But he look'd on, and smil'd, nor bar'd his sword,
But courteously drew back, and spoke, and said: —
    "Thou strik'st too hard: that club of thine will float
Upon the summer floods, and not my bones.
But rise, and be not wroth; not wroth am I:
No, when I see thee, wrath forsakes my soul.
Thou say'st, thou art not Rustum: be it so.
Who art thou then, that canst so touch my soul?
Boy as I am, I have seen battles too;
Have waded foremost in their bloody waves,
And heard their hollow roar of dying men;
But never was my heart thus touch'd before.
Are they from Heaven, these softenings of the heart?
O thou old warrior, let us yield to Heaven!
Come, plant we here in earth our angry spears,
And make a truce, and sit upon this sand,
And pledge each other in red wine, like friends,
And thou shalt talk to me of Rustum's deeds.
There are enough foes in the Persian host
Whom I may meet, and strike, and feel no pang;
Champions enough Afrasiab has, whom thou
Mayst fight; fight them, when they confront thy spear.
But oh, let there be peace 'twixt thee and me!"
    He ceas'd: but while he spake, Rustum had risen,
And stood erect, trembling with rage: his club
He left to lie, but had regain'd his spear,
Whose fiery point now in his mail'd right-hand
Blaz'd bright and baleful, like that autumn Star.
The baleful sign of fevers: dust had soil'd
His stately crest, and dimm'd his glittering arms.

His breast heav'd; his lips foam'd; and twice his voice
Was chok'd with rage: at last these words broke way: —
   "Girl! nimble with thy feet, not with thy hands!
Curl'd minion, dancer, coiner of sweet words!
Fight; let me hear thy hateful voice no more!
Thou art not in Afrasiab's gardens now
With Tartar girls, with whom thou art wont to dance;
But on the Oxus sands, and in the dance
Of battle, and with me, who make no play
Of war: I fight it out, and hand to hand.
Speak not to me of truce, and pledge, and wine!
Remember all thy valour: try thy feints
And cunning: all the pity I had is gone:
Because thou hast sham'd me before both the hosts
With thy light skipping tricks, and thy girl's wiles."
   He spoke; and Sohrab kindled at his taunts,
And he too drew his sword: at once they rush'd
Together, as two eagles on one prey
Come rushing down together from the clouds,
One from the east, one from the west: their shields
Dash'd with a clang together, and a din
Rose, such as that of the sinewy woodcutters
Make often in the forest's heart at morn,
Of hewing axes, crashing trees: such blows
Rustum and Sohrab on each other hail'd.
And you would say that sun and stars took part
In that unnatural conflict; for a cloud
Grew suddenly in Heaven, and dark'd the sun
Over the fighters' heads; and a wind rose
Under their feet, and moaning swept the plain,
And in a sandy whirlwind wrapp'd the pair.
In gloom they twain were wrapp'd, and they alone;
For both the on-looking hosts on either hand
Stood in broad daylight, and the sky was pure,
And the sun sparkled on the Oxus stream.
But in the gloom they fought, with bloodshot eyes
And labouring breath; first Rustum struck the shield
Which Sohrab held stiff out: the steel-spik'd spear
Rent the tough plates, but fail'd to reach the skin,
And Rustum pluck'd it back with angry groan.
Then Sohrab with his sword smote Rustum's helm,

Nor clove its steel quite through; but all the crest
He shore away, and that proud horsehair plume,
Never till now defil'd, sunk to the dust;
And Rustum bow'd his head; but then the gloom
Grew blacker: thunder rumbled in the air,
And lightnings rent the cloud; and Ruksh, the horse,
Who stood at hand, utter'd a dreadful cry:
No horse's cry was that, most like the roar
Of some pain'd desert lion, who all day
Has trail'd the hunter's javelin in his side,
And comes at night to die upon the sand: —
The two hosts heard that cry, and quak'd for fear,
And Oxus curdled as it cross'd his stream.
But Sohrab heard, and quail'd not, but rush'd on,
And struck again; and again Rustum bow'd
His head; but this time all the blade, like glass,
Sprang in a thousand shivers on the helm,
And in his hand the hilt remain'd alone.
Then Rustum rais'd his head: his dreadful eyes
Glar'd, and he shook on high his menacing spear,
And shouted, *Rustum!* Sohrab heard that shout,
And shrank amaz'd: back he recoil'd one step,
And scann'd with blinking eyes the advancing Form:
And then he stood bewilder'd; and he dropp'd
His covering shield, and the spear pierc'd his side.
He reel'd, and staggering back, sunk to the ground.
And then the gloom dispers'd, and the wind fell,
And the bright sun broke forth, and melted all
The cloud; and the two armies saw the pair;
Saw Rustum standing, safe upon his feet,
And Sohrab, wounded, on the bloody sand.
    Then, with a bitter smile, Rustum began: —
"Sohrab, thou thoughtest in thy mind to kill
A Persian lord this day, and strip his corpse,
And bear thy trophies to Afrasiab's tent.
Or else that the great Rustum would come down
Himself to fight, and that thy wiles would move
His heart to take a gift, and let thee go.
And then that all the Tartar host would praise
Thy courage or thy craft, and spread thy fame,
To glad thy father in his weak old age.

Fool! thou art slain, and by an unknown man!
Dearer to the red jackals shalt thou be,
Than to thy friends, and to thy father old."
    And with a fearless mien Sohrab replied: —
"Unknown thou art; yet thy fierce vaunt is vain.
Thou dost not slay me, proud and boastful man!
No! Rustum slays me, and this filial heart.
For were I match'd with ten such men as thou,
And I were he who till to-day I was,
They should be lying here. I standing there.
But that beloved name unnerv'd my arm —
That name, and something, I confess, in thee,
Which troubles all my heart, and made my shield
Fall; and thy spear transfix'd an unarm'd foe.
And now thou boastest, and insult'st my fate.
But hear thou this, fierce Man, tremble to hear!
The mighty Rustum shall avenge my death!
My father, whom I seek through all the world,
He shall avenge my death, and punish thee!"
    As when some hunter in the spring hath found
A breeding eagle sitting on her nest,
Upon the craggy isle of a hill lake,
And pierc'd her with an arrow as she rose,
And follow'd her to find her where she fell
Far off; — anon her mate comes winging back
From hunting, and a great way off descries
His huddling young left sole; at that, he checks
His pinion, and with short uneasy sweeps
Circles above his eyry, with loud screams
Chiding his mate back to her nest; but she
Lies dying, with the arrow in her side,
In some far stony gorge out of his ken,
A heap of fluttering feathers: never more
Shall the lake glass her, flying over it;
Never the black and dripping precipices
Echo her stormy scream as she sails by: —
As that poor bird flies home, nor knows his loss —
So Rustum knew not his own loss, but stood
Over his dying son, and knew him not.
    But with a cold, incredulous voice, he said: —
"What prate is this of fathers and revenge?

The mighty Rustum never had a son."
    And, with a failing voice, Sohrab replied: —
"Ah yes, he had! and that lost son am I.
Surely the news will one day reach his ear,
Reach Rustum, where he sits, and tarries long,
Somewhere, I know not where, but far from here;
And pierce him like a stab, and make him leap
To arms, and cry for vengeance upon thee.
Fierce Man, bethink thee, for an only son!
What will that grief, what will that vengeance be!
Oh, could I live, till I that grief had seen!
Yet him I pity not so much, but her,
My mother, who in Ader-baijan dwells
With that old King, her father, who grows grey
With age, and rules over the valiant Koords.
Her most I pity, who no more will see
Sohrab returning from the Tartar camp,
With spoils and honour, when the war is done.
But a dark rumour will be bruited up,
From tribe to tribe, until it reach her ear;
And then will that defenceless woman learn
That Sohrab will rejoice her sight no more;
But that in battle with a nameless foe,
By the far-distant Oxus, he is slain."
    He spoke; and as he ceas'd he wept aloud,
Thinking of her he left, and his own death.
He spoke; but Rustum listen'd, plung'd in thought.
Nor did he yet believe it was his son
Who spoke, although he call'd back names he knew;
For he had had sure tidings that the babe,
Which was in Ader-baijan born to him,
Had been a puny girl, no boy at all:
So that sad mother sent him word, for fear
Rustum should take the boy, to train in arms;
And so he deem'd that either Sohrab took,
By a false boast, the style of Rustum's son;
Or that men gave it him, to swell his fame.
So deem'd he; yet he listen'd, plung'd in thought;
And his soul set to grief, as the vast tide
Of the bright rocking Ocean sets to shore
At the full moon: tears gathered in his eyes;

For he remembered his own early youth,
And all its bounding rapture; as, at dawn,
The Shepherd from his mountain lodge descries
A far bright City, smitten by the sun,
Through many rolling clouds; — so Rustum saw
His youth; saw Sohrab's mother, in her bloom;
And that old King, her father, who lov'd well
His wandering guest, and gave him his fair child
With joy; and all the pleasant life they led,
They three, in that long-distant summer-time —
The castle, and the dewy woods, and hunt
And hound, and morn on those delightful hills
In Ader-baijan. And he saw that Youth,
Of age and looks to be his own dear son,
Piteous and lovely, lying on the sand,
Like some rich hyacinth, which by the scythe
Of an unskilful gardener has been cut,
Mowing the garden grass-plots near its bed,
And lies, a fragrant tower of purple bloom,
On the mown, dying grass; — so Sohrab lay,
Lovely in death, upon the common sand.
And Rustum gaz'd on him with grief, and said: —
    "O Sohrab, thou indeed art such a son
Whom Rustum, wert thou his, might well have lov'd!
Yet here thou errest, Sohrab, or else men
Have told thee false; — thou art not Rustum's son.
For Rustum had no son: one child he had —
But one — a girl: who with her mother now
Plies some light female task, nor dreams of us —
Of us she dreams not, nor of wounds, nor war."
    But Sohrab answer'd him in wrath; for now
The anguish of the deep-fix'd spear grew fierce,
And he desired to draw forth the steel,
And let the blood flow free, and so to die;
But first he would convince his stubborn foe —
And, rising sternly on one arm, he said: —
    "Man, who art thou who dost deny my words?
Truth sits upon the lips of dying men,
And Falsehood, while I liv'd, was far from mine.
I tell thee, prick'd upon this arm I bear
That seal which Rustum to my mother gave,

That she might prick it on the babe she bore."
    He spoke: and all the blood left Rustum's cheeks;
And his knees totter'd, and he smote his hand,
Against his breast, his heavy mailed hand,
That the hard iron corslet clank'd aloud:
And to his heart he press'd the other hand,
And in a hollow voice he spake, and said: —
    "Sohrab, that were a proof which could not lie.
If thou shew this, then art thou Rustum's son."
    Then, with weak hasty fingers, Sohrab loos'd
His belt, and near the shoulder bar'd his arm,
And shew'd a sign in faint vermilion points
Prick'd: as a cunning workman, in Pekin,
Pricks with vermilion some clear porcelain vase,
An emperor's gift — at early morn he paints,
And all day long, and, when night comes, the lamp
Lights up his studious forehead and thin hands: —
So delicately prick'd the sign appear'd
On Sohrab's arm, the sign of Rustum's seal.
It was that Griffin, which of old rear'd Zal,
Rustum's great father, whom they left to die,
A helpless babe, among the mountain rocks.
Him that kind Creature found, and rear'd, and lov'd —
Then Rustum took it for his glorious sign.
And Sohrab bar'd that figure on his arm,
And himself scann'd it long with mournful eyes,
And then he touch'd it with his hand and said: —
    "How say'st thou? Is that sign the proper sign
Of Rustum's son, or of some other man's?"
    He spoke: but Rustum gaz'd, and gaz'd, and stood
Speechless; and then he utter'd one sharp cry —
O Boy — thy Father! — and his voice choked there.
And then a dark cloud pass'd before his eyes,
And his head swam, and he sunk down to earth.
But Sohrab crawl'd to where he lay, and cast
His arms about his neck, and kiss'd his lips,
And with fond faltering fingers strok'd his cheeks,
Trying to call him back to life: and life
Came back to Rustum, and he op'd his eyes
And they stood wide with horror; and he seiz'd
In both his hands the dust which lay around,

And threw it on his head, and smirch'd his hair,
His hair, and face, and beard, and glittering arms:
And strong convulsive groanings shook his breast,
And his sobs chok'd him; and he clutch'd his sword,
To draw it, and for ever let life out.
But Sohrab saw his thought, and held his hands,
And with a soothing voice he spoke, and said: —
   "Father, forbear: for I but meet to-day
The doom that at my birth was written down
In Heaven, and thou art Heaven's unconscious hand.
Surely my heart cried out that it was thou,
When first I saw thee; and thy heart spoke too,
I know it: but Fate trod those promptings down
Under its iron heel; Fate, Fate engag'd
The strife and hurl'd me on my father's spear.
But let us speak no more of this: I find
My father; let me feel that I have found.
Come, sit beside me on this sand, and take
My head betwixt thy hands, and kiss my cheeks,
And wash them with thy tears, and say, 'My Son!'
Quick! quick! for number'd are my sands of life,
And swift; for like the lightning to this field
I came, and like the wind I go away —
Sudden, and swift, and like a passing wind.
But it was writ in Heaven that this should be."
   So said he: and his voice releas'd the heart
Of Rustum, and his tears broke forth; he cast
His arms round his son's neck, and wept aloud,
And kiss'd him. And awe fell on both the hosts
When they saw Rustum's grief: and Ruksh, the horse,
With his head bowing to the ground, and mane
Sweeping the dust, came near, and in mute woe
First to the one then to the other mov'd
His head, as if enquiring what their grief
Might mean; and from his dark, compassionate eyes,
The big warm tears roll'd down, and cak'd the sand.
But Rustum chid him with stern voice, and said: —
   "Ruksh, now thou grievest; but, O Ruksh, thy feet
Should then have rotted on their nimble joints,
When first they bore thy Master to this field."
   But Sohrab look'd upon the horse and said: —

"Is this then Ruksh? How often, in past days,
My mother told me of thee, thou brave Steed!
My terrible father's terrible horse; and said,
That I should one day find thy lord and thee.
Come, let me lay my hand upon thy mane.
O Ruksh, thou art more fortunate than I;
For thou hast gone where I shall never go,
And snuff'd the breezes of my father's home.
And thou hast trod the sands of Seistan,
And seen the River of Helmund, and the Lake
Of Zirrah; and the aged Zal himself
Has often strok'd thy neck, and given thee food,
Corn in a golden platter soak'd with wine,
And said — 'O Ruksh! bear Rustum well!' — but I
Have never known my grandsire's furrow'd face,
Nor seen his lofty house in Seistan,
Nor slak'd my thirst at the clear Helmund stream:
But lodg'd among my father's foes, and seen
Afrasiab's cities only, Samarcand,
Bokhara, and lone Khiva in the waste,
And the black Toorkmun tents; and only drunk
The desert rivers, Moorghab and Tejend,
Kohik, and where the Kalmuks feed their sheep,
The northern Sir; and this great Oxus stream —
The yellow Oxus, by whose brink I die."
     And, with a heavy groan, Rustum replied: —
"Oh that its waves were flowing over me!
Oh that I saw its grains of yellow silt
Roll tumbling in the current o'er my head!"
     And, with a grave mild voice, Sohrab replied: —
"Desire not that, my father; thou must live.
For some are born to do great deeds, and live,
As some are born to be obscur'd, and die.
Do thou the deeds I die too young to do,
And reap a second glory in thine age.
Thou art my father, and thy gain is mine.
But come: thou seest this great host of men
Which follow me; I pray thee, slay not these:
Let me entreat for them: what have they done?
They follow'd me, my hope, my fame, my star.
Let them all cross the Oxus back in peace.

But me thou must bear hence, not send with them,
But carry me with thee to Seistan,
And place me on a bed, and mourn for me,
Thou, and the snow-hair'd Zal, and all thy friends.
And thou must lay me in that lovely earth,
And heap a stately mound above my bones,
And plant a far-seen pillar over all:
That so the passing horseman on the waste
May see my tomb a great way off, and say —
Sohrab, the mighty Rustum's son, lies there,
Whom his great father did in ignorance kill —
And I be not forgotten in my grave."
    And, with a mournful voice, Rustum replied: —
"Fear not; as thou hast said, Sohrab, my son,
So shall it be: for I will burn my tents,
And quit the host, and bear thee hence with me,
And carry thee away to Seistan,
And place thee on a bed, and mourn for thee,
With the snow-headed Zal, and all my friends.
And I will lay thee in that lovely earth,
And heap a stately mound above thy bones,
And plant a far-seen pillar over all:
And men shall not forget thee in thy grave.
And I will spare thy host: yea, let them go:
Let them all cross the Oxus back in peace.
What should I do with slaying any more?
For would that all whom I have ever slain
Might be once more alive; my bitterest foes,
And they who were call'd champions in their time,
And through whose death I won that fame I have;
And I were nothing but a common man,
A poor, mean soldier, and without renown;
So thou mightest live too, my Son, my Son!
Or rather would that I, even I myself,
Might now be lying on this bloody sand,
Near death, and by an ignorant stroke of thine,
Not thou of mine; and I might die, not thou;
And I, not thou, be borne to Seistan;
And Zal might weep above my grave, not thine;
And say — *O son, I weep thee not too sore,*
For willingly, I know, thou met'st thine end. —

But now in blood and battles was my youth,
And full of blood and battles is my age;
And I shall never end this life of blood."
    Then, at the point of death, Sohrab replied: —
"A life of blood indeed, thou dreadful Man!
But thou shalt yet have peace; only not now;
Not yet: but thou shalt have it on that day,
When thou shalt sail in a high-masted Ship,
Thou and the other peers of Kai-Khosroo,
Returning home over the salt blue sea,
From laying thy dear Master in his grave."
    And Rustum gaz'd on Sohrab's face, and said: —
"Soon be that day, my Son, and deep that sea!
Till then, if Fate so wills, let me endure."
    He spoke; and Sohrab smil'd on him, and took
The spear, and drew it from his side, and eas'd
His wound's imperious anguish: but the blood
Came welling from the open gash, and life
Flow'd with the stream: all down his cold white side
The crimson torrent ran, dim now, and soil'd,
Like the soil'd tissue of white violets
Left, freshly gather'd, on their native bank,
By romping children, whom their nurses call
From the hot fields at noon: his head droop'd low
His limbs grew slack; motionless, white, he lay —
White, with eyes clos'd; only when heavy gasps,
Deep, heavy gasps, quivering through all his frame,
Convuls'd him back to life, he open'd them,
And fix'd them feebly on his father's face:
Till now all strength was ebb'd, and from his limbs
Unwillingly the spirit fled away,
Regretting the warm mansion which it left,
And youth and bloom, and this delightful world.
    So, on the bloody sand, Sohrab lay dead.
And the great Rustum drew his horseman's cloak
Down o'er his face, and sate by his dead son.
As those black granite pillars, once high-rear'd
By Jemshid in Persepolis, to bear
His house, now, mid their broken flights of steps,
Lie prone, enormous, down the mountain side —
So in the sand lay Rustum by his son.

And night came down over the solemn waste,
And the two gazing hosts, and that sole pair,
And darken'd all; and a cold fog, with night,
Crept from the Oxus. Soon a hum arose,
As of a great assembly loos'd, and fires
Began to twinkle through the fog: for now
Both armies mov'd to camp, and took their meal:
The Persians took it on the open sands
Southward; the Tartars by the river marge:
And Rustum and his son were left alone.

But the majestic River floated on,
Out of the mist and hum of that low land,
Into the frosty starlight, and there mov'd,
Rejoicing, through the hush'd Chorasmian waste,
Under the solitary moon: he flow'd
Right for the Polar Star, past Orgunjè,
Brimming, and bright, and large: then sands begin
To hem his watery march, and dam his streams,
And split his currents; that for many a league
The shorn and parcell'd Oxus strains along
Through beds of sand and matted rushy isles —
Oxus, forgetting the bright speed he had
In his high mountain cradle in Pamere,
A foil'd circuitous wanderer: — till at last
The long'd-for dash of waves is heard, and wide
His luminous home of waters opens, bright
And tranquil, from whose floor the new-bath'd stars
Emerge, and shine upon the Aral Sea.

Requiescat

Strew on her roses, roses,
    And never a spray of yew.
In quiet she reposes:
    Ah! would that I did too.

Her mirth the world required:
    She bath'd it in smiles of glee.
But her heart was tired, tired,
    And now they let her be.

Her life was turning, turning,
    In mazes of heat and sound.
But for peace her soul was yearning,
    And now peace laps her round.

Her cabin'd, ample Spirit,
    It flutter'd and fail'd for breath.
To-night it doth inherit
    The vasty Hall of Death.

Stanzas from the Grande Chartreuse

Through Alpine meadows, soft-suffused
With rain, where thick the crocus blows,
Past the dark forges long disused,
The mule-track from Saint Laurent goes.
The bridge is cross'd, and slow we ride,
Through forest, up the mountain-side.

The autumnal evening darkens round,
The wind is up, and drives the rain;
While hark! far down, with strangled sound
Doth the Dead Guiers' stream complain,
Where that wet smoke among the woods
Over his boiling cauldron broods.

Swift rush the spectral vapours white
Past limestone scars with ragged pines,
Showing — then blotting from our sight.
Halt! through the cloud-drift something shines!
High in the valley, wet and drear,
The huts of Courrerie appear.

Strike leftward! cries our guide; and higher
Mounts up the stony forest-way.
At last the encircling trees retire;
Look! through the showery twilight grey
What pointed roofs are these advance?
A palace of the Kings of France?

Approach, for what we seek is here.
Alight and sparely sup and wait

For rest in this outbuilding near;
Then cross the sward and reach that gate;
Knock; pass the wicket! Thou art come
To the Carthusians' world-famed home.

The silent courts, where night and day
Into their stone-carved basins cold
The splashing icy fountains play,
The humid corridors behold,
Where ghostlike in the deepening night
Cowl'd forms brush by in gleaming white:

The chapel, where no organ's peal
Invests the stern and naked prayer.
With penitential cries they kneel
And wrestle; rising then, with bare
And white uplifted faces stand,
Passing the Host from hand to hand;

Each takes; and then his visage wan
Is buried in his cowl once more.
The cells—the suffering Son of Man
Upon the wall! the knee-worn floor!
And, where they sleep, that wooden bed,
Which shall their coffin be, when dead.

The library, where tract and tome
Not to feed priestly pride are there,
To hymn the conquering march of Rome,
Nor yet to amuse, as ours are;
They paint of souls the inner strife,
Their drops of blood, their death in life.

The garden, overgrown—yet mild
Those fragrant herbs are flowering there!
Strong children of the Alpine wild
Whose culture is the brethren's care;
Of human tasks their only one,
And cheerful works beneath the sun.

Those halls too, destined to contain
Each its own pilgrim host of old,
From England, Germany, or Spain—
All are before me! I behold

The House, the Brotherhood austere!
And what am I, that I am here?

For rigorous teachers seized my youth,
And purged its faith, and trimm'd its fire,
Show'd me the high white star of Truth,
There bade me gaze, and there aspire;
Even now their whispers pierce the gloom:
What dost thou in this living tomb?

Forgive me, masters of the mind!
At whose behest I long ago
So much unlearnt, so much resign'd!
I come not here to be your foe.
I seek these anchorites, not in ruth,
To curse and to deny your truth;

Not as their friend or child I speak!
But as on some far northern strand,
Thinking of his own Gods, a Greek
In pity and mournful awe might stand
Before some fallen Runic stone —
For both were faiths, and both are gone.

Wandering between two worlds, one dead,
The other powerless to be born,
With nowhere yet to rest my head,
Like these, on earth I wait forlorn.
Their faith, my tears, the world deride;
I come to shed them at their side.

Oh, hide me in your gloom profound,
Ye solemn seats of holy pain!
Take me, cowl'd forms, and fence me round,
Till I possess my soul again!
Till free my thoughts before me roll,
Not chafed by hourly false control.

For the world cries your faith is now
But a dead time's exploded dream;
My melancholy, sciolists say,
Is a pass'd mode, an outworn theme —
As if the world had ever had
A faith, or sciolists been sad.

Ah, if it *be* pass'd, take away,
At least, the restlessness — the pain!
Be man henceforth no more a prey
To these out-dated stings again!
The nobleness of grief is gone —
Ah, leave us not the fret alone!

But, if you cannot give us ease,
Last of the race of them who grieve
Here leave us to die out with these
Last of the people who believe!
Silent, while years engrave the brow;
Silent — the best are silent now.

Achilles ponders in his tent,
The kings of modern thought are dumb;
Silent they are, though not content,
And wait to see the future come.
They have the grief men had of yore,
But they contend and cry no more.

Our fathers water'd with their tears
This sea of time whereon we sail;
Their voices were in all men's ears
Who pass'd within their puissant hail.
Still the same Ocean round us raves,
But we stand mute, and watch the waves.

For what avail'd it, all the noise
And outcry of the former men?
Say, have their sons obtain'd more joys?
Say, is life lighter now than then?
The sufferers died, they left their pain;
The pangs which tortured them remain.

What helps it now, that Byron bore,
With haughty scorn which mock'd the smart,
Through Europe to the Aetolian shore
The pageant of his bleeding heart?
That thousands counted every groan,
And Europe made his woe her own?

What boots it, Shelley! that the breeze
Carried thy lovely wail away,

Musical through Italian trees
That fringe thy soft blue Spezzian bay?
Inheritors of thy distress
Have restless hearts one throb the less?

Or are we easier, to have read,
O Obermann! the sad, stern page,
Which tells us how thou hidd'st thy head
From the fierce tempest of thine age
In the lone brakes of Fontainebleau,
Or chalets near the Alpine snow?

Ye slumber in your silent grave!
The world, which for an idle day
Grace to your mood of sadness gave,
Long since hath flung her weeds away.
The eternal trifler breaks your spell;
But we — we learnt your lore too well!

There may, perhaps, yet dawn an age,
More fortunate, alas! than we,
Which without hardness will be sage,
And gay without frivolity.
Sons of the world, oh, haste those years;
But, till they rise, allow our tears!

Allow them! We admire with awe
The exulting thunder of your race;
You give the universe your law,
You triumph over time and space.
Your pride of life, your tireless powers,
We mark them, but they are not ours.

We are like children rear'd in shade
Beneath some old-world abbey wall
Forgotten in a forest-glade
And secret from the eyes of all;
Deep, deep the greenwood round them waves,
Their abbey, and its close of graves.

But, where the road runs near the stream,
Oft through the trees they catch a glance
Of passing troops in the sun's beam —
Pennon, and plume, and flashing lance!

Forth to the world those soldiers fare,
To life, to cities, and to war.

And through the woods, another way,
Faint bugle-notes from far are borne,
Where hunters gather, staghounds bay,
Round some old forest-lodge at morn;
Gay dames are there in sylvan green,
Laughter and cries — those notes between!

The banners flashing through the trees
Make their blood dance and chain their eyes;
That bugle-music on the breeze
Arrests them with a charm'd surprise.
Banner by turns and bugle woo:
Ye shy recluses, follow too!

O children, what do ye reply? —
"Action and pleasure, will ye roam
Through these secluded dells to cry
And call us? but too late ye come!
Too late for us your call ye blow
Whose bent was taken long ago.

"Long since we pace this shadow'd nave;
We watch those yellow tapers shine,
Emblems of hope over the grave,
In the high altar's depth divine;
The organ carries to our ear
Its accents of another sphere.

"Fenced early in this cloistral round
Of reverie, of shade, of prayer,
How should we grow in other ground?
How should we flower in foreign air?
Pass, banners, pass, and bugles, cease!
And leave our desert to its peace!"

To Marguerite

We were apart! yet, day by day,
I bade my heart more constant be;
I bade it keep the world away,
And grow a home for only thee;
Nor fear'd but thy love likewise grew.
Like mine, each day more tried, more true.

The fault was grave! I might have known,
What far too soon, alas! I learn'd —
The heart can bind itself alone,
And faith is often unreturn'd.
Self-sway'd our feelings ebb and swell!
Thou lov'st no more; — Farewell! Farewell!

Farewell! — and thou, thou lonely heart,
Which never yet without remorse
Even for a moment didst depart
From thy remote and spheréd course
To haunt the place where passions reign —
Back to thy solitude again!

Back! with the conscious thrill of shame
Which Luna felt, that summer-night,
Flash through her pure immortal frame,
When she forsook the starry height
To hang over Endymion's sleep
Upon the pine-grown Latmian steep —

Yet she, chaste queen, had never proved
How vain a thing is mortal love,
Wandering in Heaven, far removed;
But thou hast long had place to prove
This truth — to prove, and make thine own:
"Thou hast been, shalt be, art, alone."

Or, if not quite alone, yet they
Which touch thee are unmating things —
Ocean and clouds and night and day;
Lorn autumns and triumphant springs;

And life, and others' joy and pain,
And love, if love, of happier men.

Of happier men! — for they, at least,
Have dream'd two human hearts might blend
In one, and were through faith released
From isolation without end
Prolong'd; nor knew, although not less
Alone than thou, their loneliness!

A Southern Night

The sandy spits, the shore-lock'd lakes,
   Melt into open, moonlit sea;
The soft Mediterranean breaks
     At my feet, free.

Dotting the fields of corn and vine
   Like ghosts, the huge, gnarl'd olives stand;
Behind, that lovely mountain-line!
     While by the strand

Cette, with its glistening houses white,
   Curves with the curving beach away
To where the lighthouse beacons bright
     Far in the bay.

Ah, such a night, so soft, so lone,
   So moonlit, saw me once of yore
Wander unquiet, and my own
     Vext heart deplore!

But now that trouble is forgot;
   Thy memory, thy pain, to-night,
My brother! and thine early lot,
     Possess me quite.

The murmur of this Midland deep
   Is heard to-night around thy grave
There, where Gibraltar's cannon'd steep
     O'erfrowns the wave.

For there, with bodily anguish keen,
  With Indian heats at last fordone,
With public toil and private teen,
      Thou sank'st, alone.

Slow to a stop, at morning grey,
  I see the smoke-crown'd vessel come;
Slow round her paddles dies away
      The seething foam.

A boat is lower'd from her side;
  Ah, gently place him on the bench!
That spirit — if all have not yet died —
      A breath might quench.

Is this the eye, the footstep fast,
  The mien of youth we used to see,
Poor, gallant boy! — for such thou wast,
      Still art, to me.

The limbs their wonted tasks refuse,
  The eyes are glazed, thou canst not speak;
And whiter than thy white burnous
      That wasted cheek!

Enough! The boat, with quiet shock,
  Unto its haven coming nigh,
Touches, and on Gibraltar's rock
      Lands thee, to die.

Ah me! Gibraltar's strand is far,
  But farther yet across the brine
Thy dear wife's ashes buried are,
      Remote from thine.

For there where Morning's sacred fount
  Its golden rain on earth confers,
The snowy Himalayan Mount
      O'ershadows hers.

Strange irony of Fate, alas,
  Which for two jaded English saves,
When from their dusty life they pass,
      Such peaceful graves!

In cities should we English lie,
  Where cries are rising ever new,
And men's incessant stream goes by;
    We who pursue

Our business with unslackening stride,
  Traverse in troops, with care-fill'd breast,
The soft Mediterranean side,
    The Nile, the East,

And see all sights from pole to pole,
  And glance, and nod, and bustle by;
And never once possess our soul
    Before we die.

Not by those hoary Indian hills,
  Not by this gracious Midland sea
Whose floor to-night sweet moonshine fills,
    Should our graves be!

Some sage, to whom the world was dead,
  And men were specks, and life a play;
Who made the roots of trees his bed,
    And once a day

With staff and gourd his way did bend
  To villages and homes of man,
For food to keep him till he end
    His mortal span,

And the pure goal of Being reach;
  Grey-headed, wrinkled, clad in white,
Without companion, without speech,
    By day and night

Pondering God's mysteries untold,
  And tranquil as the glacier snows —
He by those Indian mountains old
    Might well repose!

Some grey crusading knight austere,
  Who bore Saint Louis company
And came home hurt to death and here
    Landed to die;

Some youthful troubadour whose tongue
    Fill'd Europe once with his love-pain,
Who here outwearied sunk, and sung
        His dying strain;

Some girl who here from castle-bower,
    With furtive step and cheek of flame,
'Twixt myrtle-hedges all in flower
        By moonlight came

To meet her pirate-lover's ship,
    And from the wave-kiss'd marble stair
Beckon'd him on, with quivering lip
        And unbound hair,

And lived some moons in happy trance,
    Then learnt his death, and pined away—
Such by these waters of romance
        'Twas meet to lay!

But you—a grave for knight or sage,
    Romantic, solitary, still,
O spent ones of a work-day age!
        Befits you ill.

So sang I; but the midnight breeze
    Down to the brimm'd moon-charmed main
Comes softly through the olive-trees,
        And checks my strain.

I think of her, whose gentle tongue
    All plaint in her own cause controll'd;
Of thee I think, my brother! young
        In heart, high-soul'd;

That comely face, that cluster'd brow,
    That cordial hand, that bearing free,
I see them still, I see them now,
        Shall always see!

And what but gentleness untired,
    And what but noble feeling warm,
Wherever shown, howe'er attired,
        Is grace, is charm?

What else is all these waters are,
　What else is steep'd in lucid sheen,
What else is bright, what else is fair,
　　What else serene?

Mild o'er her grave, ye mountains, shine!
　Gently by his, ye waters, glide!
To that in you which is divine
　　They were allied.

Thyrsis

A MONODY, *to commemorate the author's friend,* ARTHUR
　HUGH CLOUGH, *who died at Florence,* 1861

　　Thus yesterday, to-day, to-morrow come,
　　They hustle one another and they pass;
　　But all our hustling morrows only make
　　The smooth to-day of God.
　　　　　From Lucretius, *an unpublished Tragedy.*

How changed is here each spot man makes or fills!
　In the two Hinkseys nothing keeps the same;
　　The village-street its haunted mansion lacks,
　And from the sign is gone Sibylla's name,
　　And from the roofs the twisted chimney-stacks;
　　　Are ye too changed, ye hills?
　See, 'tis no foot of unfamiliar men
　　To-night from Oxford up your pathway strays!
　　Here came I often, often, in old days;
　Thyrsis and I; we still had Thyrsis then.

Runs it not here, the track by Childsworth Farm,
　Up past the wood, to where the elm-tree crowns
　　The hill behind whose ridge the sunset flames?
　The signal-elm, that looks on Ilsley Downs,
　　The Vale, the three lone weirs, the youthful Thames? —
　　　This winter-eve is warm,
　Humid the air; leafless, yet soft as spring,
　　The tender purple spray on copse and briers;

And that sweet City with her dreaming spires,
She needs not June for beauty's heightening,

Lovely all times she lies, lovely to-night!
   Only, methinks, some loss of habit's power
      Befalls me wandering through this upland dim;
   Once pass'd I blindfold here, at any hour,
      Now seldom come I, since I came with him.
         That single elm-tree bright
   Against the west—I miss it! is it gone?
      We prized it dearly; while it stood, we said,
      Our friend, the Scholar-Gipsy, was not dead;
   While the tree lived, he in these fields lived on.

Too rare, too rare, grow now my visits here!
   But once I knew each field, each flower, each stick;
      And with the country-folk acquaintance made
   By barn in threshing-time, by new-built rick.
      Here, too, our shepherd-pipes we first assay'd.
         Ah me! this many a year
   My pipe is lost, my shepherd's-holiday!
      Needs must I lose them, needs with heavy heart
      Into the world and wave of men depart;
   But Thyrsis of his own will went away.

It irk'd him to be here, he could not rest.
   He loved each simple joy the country yields,
      He loved his mates; but yet he could not keep,
   For that a shadow lower'd on the fields,
      Here with the shepherds and the silly sheep.
         Some life of men unblest
   He knew, which made him droop, and fill'd his head.
      He went; his piping took a troubled sound
      Of storms that rage outside our happy ground;
   He could not wait their passing, he is dead!

So, some tempestuous morn in early June,
   When the year's primal burst of bloom is o'er,
      Before the roses and the longest day—
   When garden-walks, and all the grassy floor,
      With blossoms, red and white, of fallen May,
         And chestnut-flowers are strewn—
   So have I heard the cuckoo's parting cry,

From the wet field, through the vext garden-trees,
  Come with the volleying rain and tossing breeze:
The bloom is gone, and with the bloom go I.

Too quick despairer, wherefore wilt thou go?
  Soon will the high Midsummer pomps come on,
    Soon will the musk carnations break and swell,
  Soon shall we have gold-dusted snapdragon,
    Sweet-William with its homely cottage-smell,
      And stocks in fragrant blow;
  Roses that down the alleys shine afar,
    And open, jasmine-muffled lattices,
    And groups under the dreaming garden-trees,
  And the full moon, and the white evening-star.

He hearkens not! light comer, he is flown!
  What matters it? next year he will return,
    And we shall have him in the sweet spring-days,
  With whitening hedges, and uncrumpling fern,
    And blue-bells trembling by the forest-ways,
      And scent of hay new-mown.
  But Thyrsis never more we swains shall see!
    See him come back, and cut a smoother reed,
    And blow a strain the world at last shall heed —
  For Time, not Corydon, hath conquer'd thee.

Alack, for Corydon no rival now! —
  But when Sicilian shepherds lost a mate,
    Some good survivor with his flute would go,
  Piping a ditty sad for Bion's fate,
    And cross the unpermitted ferry's flow,
      And relax Pluto's brow,
  And make leap up with joy the beauteous head
    Of Proserpine, among whose crowned hair
    Are flowers, first open'd on Sicilian air,
  And flute his friend, like Orpheus, from the dead.

O easy access to the hearer's grace
  When Dorian shepherds sang to Proserpine!
    For she herself had trod Sicilian fields,
  She knew the Dorian water's gush divine,
    She knew each lily white which Enna yields,
      Each rose with blushing face;

She loved the Dorian pipe, the Dorian strain.
  But ah, of our poor Thames she never heard!
  Her foot the Cumnor cowslips never stirr'd!
And we should tease her with our plaint in vain.

Well! wind-dispers'd and vain the words will be,
  Yet, Thyrsis, let me give my grief its hour
    In the old haunt, and find our tree-topp'd hill!
  Who, if not I, for questing here hath power?
    I know the wood which hides the daffodil,
      I know the Fyfield tree,
  I know what white, what purple fritillaries
    The grassy harvest of the river-fields,
    Above by Ensham, down by Sandford, yields,
And what sedg'd brooks are Thames's tributaries;

I know these slopes; who knows them if not I? —
  But many a dingle on the loved hill-side,
    With thorns once studded, old, white-blossom'd trees,
  Where thick the cowslips grew, and, far descried,
    High tower'd the spikes of purple orchises,
      Hath since our day put by
  The coronals of that forgotten time.
    Down each green bank hath gone the ploughboy's team,
    And only in the hidden brookside gleam
  Primroses, orphans of the flowery prime.

Where is the girl, who, by the boatman's door,
  Above the locks, above the boating throng,
    Unmoor'd our skiff, when, through the Wytham flats,
  Red loosestrife and blond meadow-sweet among,
    And darting swallows, and light water-gnats,
      We track'd the shy Thames shore?
  Where are the mowers, who, as the tiny swell
    Of our boat passing heav'd the river-grass,
    Stood with suspended scythe to see us pass? —
  They all are gone, and thou art gone as well.

Yes, thou art gone! and round me too the night
  In ever-nearing circle weaves her shade.
    I see her veil draw soft across the day,
  I feel her slowly chilling breath invade
    The cheek grown thin, the brown hair sprent with grey;

I feel her finger light
Laid pausefully upon life's headlong train;
    The foot less prompt to meet the morning dew,
    The heart less bounding at emotion new,
And hope, once crush'd, less quick to spring again.

And long the way appears, which seem'd so short
    To the unpractis'd eye of sanguine youth;
        And high the mountain-tops, in cloudy air,
    The mountain-tops where is the throne of Truth,
        Tops in life's morning-sun so bright and bare!
            Unbreachable the fort
Of the long-batter'd world uplifts its wall.
    And strange and vain the earthly turmoil grows,
    And near and real the charm of thy repose,
And night as welcome as a friend would fall.

But hush! the upland hath a sudden loss
    Of quiet; — Look! adown the dusk hillside,
    A troop of Oxford hunters going home,
As in old days, jovial and talking, ride!
    From hunting with the Berkshire hounds they come —
        Quick, let me fly, and cross
Into yon further field! — 'Tis done; and see,
    Back'd by the sunset, which doth glorify
    The orange and pale violet evening-sky,
Bare on its lonely ridge, the Tree! the Tree!

I take the omen! Eve lets down her veil,
    The white fog creeps from bush to bush about,
        The west unflushes, the high stars grow bright,
    And in the scatter'd farms the lights come out.
        I cannot reach the Signal-Tree to-night,
            Yet, happy omen, hail!
    Hear it from thy broad lucent Arno vale
        (For there thine earth-forgetting eyelids keep
        The morningless and unawakening sleep
    Under the flowery oleanders pale),

Hear it, O Thyrsis, still our Tree is there! —
    Ah, vain! These English fields, this upland dim,
        These brambles pale with mist engarlanded,
    That lone, sky-pointing tree, are not for him.

To a boon southern country he is fled,
    And now in happier air,
Wandering with the great Mother's train divine
    (And purer or more subtle soul than thee,
    I trow, the mighty Mother doth not see!)
Within a folding of the Apennine,

Thou hearest the immortal strains of old.
    Putting his sickle to the perilous grain
      In the hot cornfield of the Phrygian king,
    For thee the Lityerses song again
      Young Daphnis with his silver voice doth sing;
        Sings his Sicilian fold,
    His sheep, his hapless love, his blinded eyes;
      And how a call celestial round him rang
      And heavenward from the fountain-brink he sprang,
And all the marvel of the golden skies.

There thou art gone, and me thou leavest here
    Sole in these fields; yet will I not despair;
      Despair I will not, while I yet descry
    'Neath the soft canopy of English air
      That lonely Tree against the western sky.
        Still, still these slopes, 'tis clear,
    Our Gipsy-Scholar haunts, outliving thee!
      Fields where soft sheep from cages pull the hay,
      Woods with anemonies in flower till May,
Know him a wanderer still; then why not me?

A fugitive and gracious light he seeks,
    Shy to illumine; and I seek it too.
      This does not come with houses or with gold,
    With place, with honour, and a flattering crew;
      'Tis not in the world's market bought and sold.
        But the smooth-slipping weeks
    Drop by, and leave its seeker still untired;
      Out of the heed of mortals he is gone,
      He wends unfollow'd, he must house alone;
Yet on he fares, by his own heart inspired.

Thou too, O Thyrsis, on like quest wert bound,
    Thou wanderedst with me for a little hour;
      Men gave thee nothing, but this happy quest,

    If men esteem'd thee feeble, gave thee power,
      If men procured thee trouble, gave thee rest.
        And this rude Cumnor ground,
    Its fir-topped Hurst, its farms, its quiet fields,
      Here cam'st thou in thy jocund youthful time,
      Here was thine height of strength, thy golden prime;
    And still the haunt beloved a virtue yields.

What though the music of thy rustic flute
    Kept not for long its happy, country tone,
      Lost it too soon, and learnt a stormy note
Of men contention-tost, of men who groan,
      Which task'd thy pipe too sore, and tired thy throat —
        It fail'd, and thou wast mute;
Yet hadst thou always visions of our light,
    And long with men of care thou couldst not stay,
     And soon thy foot resumed its wandering way,
Left human haunt, and on alone till night.

Too rare, too rare, grow now my visits here!
    'Mid city-noise, not, as with thee of yore,
      Thyrsis, in reach of sheep-bells is my home!
Then through the great town's harsh, heart-wearying roar,
    Let in thy voice a whisper often come,
        To chase fatigue and fear:
    Why faintest thou? I wander'd till I died.
    Roam on! the light we sought is shining still.
    Dost thou ask proof? Our Tree yet crowns the hill,
Our Scholar travels yet the loved hillside.

Dover Beach

The sea is calm to-night,
The tide is full, the moon lies fair
Upon the Straits; — on the French coast, the light
Gleams, and is gone; the cliffs of England stand,
Glimmering and vast, out in the tranquil bay.
Come to the window, sweet is the night air!
Only, from the long line of spray
Where the ebb meets the moon-blanch'd sand,

Listen! you hear the grating roar
Of pebbles which the waves suck back, and fling,
At their return, up the high strand,
Begin, and cease, and then again begin,
With tremulous cadence slow, and bring
The eternal note of sadness in.

Sophocles long ago
Heard it on the Aegaean, and it brought
Into his mind the turbid ebb and flow
Of human misery; we
Find also in the sound a thought,
Hearing it by this distant northern sea.

The sea of faith
Was once, too, at the full, and round earth's shore
Lay like the folds of a bright girdle furl'd;
But now I only hear
Its melancholy, long, withdrawing roar,
Retreating to the breath
Of the night-wind down the vast edges drear
And naked shingles of the world.

Ah, love, let us be true
To one another! for the world, which seems
To lie before us like a land of dreams,
So various, so beautiful, so new,
Hath really neither joy, nor love, nor light,
Nor certitude, nor peace, nor help for pain;
And we are here as on a darkling plain
Swept with confused alarms of struggle and flight,
Where ignorant armies clash by night.

Immortality

Foil'd by our fellow men, depress'd, outworn,
We leave the brutal world to take its way,
And, *Patience! in another life*, we say,
The world shall be thrust down, and we up-borne!

And will not, then, the immortal armies scorn
The world's poor, routed leavings; or will they,

Who fail'd under the heat of this life's day,
Support the fervours of the heavenly morn?

No, no! the energy of life may be
Kept on after the grave, but not begun;
And he who flagg'd not in the earthly strife,

From strength to strength advancing — only he,
His soul well-knit, and all his battles won,
Mounts, and that hardly, to eternal life.

Rugby Chapel

NOVEMBER, 1857

Coldly, sadly descends
The autumn evening. The Field
Strewn with its dank yellow drifts
Of wither'd leaves, and the elms,
Fade into dimness apace,
Silent; — hardly a shout
From a few boys late at their play!
The lights come out in the street,
In the school-room windows; but cold,
Solemn, unlighted, austere,
Through the gathering darkness, arise
The Chapel walls, in whose bound
Thou, my father! art laid.

There thou dost lie, in the gloom
Of the autumn evening. But ah!
That word, *gloom*, to my mind
Brings thee back in the light
Of thy radiant vigour again!
In the gloom of November we pass'd
Days not of gloom at thy side;
Seasons impair'd not the ray
Of thine even cheerfulness clear.
Such thou wast; and I stand
In the autumn evening, and think
Of bygone autumns with thee.

Fifteen years have gone round
Since thou arosest to tread,
In the summer morning, the road
Of death, at a call unforeseen,
Sudden. For fifteen years,
We who till then in thy shade
Rested as under the boughs
Of a mighty oak, have endured
Sunshine and rain as we might,
Bare, unshaded, alone,
Lacking the shelter of thee.

O strong soul, by what shore
Tarriest thou now? For that force,
Surely, has not been left vain!
Somewhere, surely, afar,
In the sounding labour-house vast
Of being, is practised that strength,
Zealous, beneficent, firm!

Yes, in some far-shining sphere,
Conscious or not of the past,
Still thou performest the word
Of the Spirit in whom thou dost live,
Prompt, unwearied, as here!
Still thou upraisest with zeal
The humble good from the ground,
Sternly repressest the bad.
Still, like a trumpet, dost rouse
Those who with half-open eyes
Tread the border-land dim
'Twixt vice and virtue; reviv'st,
Succourest; — this was thy work,
This was thy life upon earth.

What is the course of the life
Of mortal men on the earth? —
Most men eddy about
Here and there — eat and drink,
Chatter and love and hate,
Gather and squander, are raised
Aloft, are hurl'd in the dust,
Striving blindly, achieving

Nothing, and then they die —
Perish; and no one asks
Who or what they have been,
More than he asks what waves
In the moonlit solitudes mild
Of the midmost Ocean, have swell'd,
Foam'd for a moment, and gone.

And there are some, whom a thirst
Ardent, unquenchable, fires,
Not with the crowd to be spent,
Not without aim to go round
In an eddy of purposeless dust,
Effort unmeaning and vain.
Ah yes, some of us strive
Not without action to die
Fruitless, but something to snatch
From dull oblivion, nor all
Glut the devouring grave!
We, we have chosen our path —
Path to a clear-purposed goal,
Path of advance! but it leads
A long, steep journey, through sunk
Gorges, o'er mountains in snow!
Cheerful, with friends, we set forth;
Then, on the height, comes the storm!
Thunder crashes from rock
To rock, the cataracts reply;
Lightnings dazzle our eyes;
Roaring torrents have breach'd
The track, the stream-bed descends
In the place where the wayfarer once
Planted his footstep — the spray
Boils o'er its borders; aloft,
The unseen snow-beds dislodge
Their hanging ruin; — alas,
Havoc is made in our train!
Friends who set forth at our side
Falter, are lost in the storm!
We, we only, are left!
With frowning foreheads, with lips

Sternly compress'd, we strain on,
On — and at nightfall, at last,
Come to the end of our way,
To the lonely inn 'mid the rocks;
Where the gaunt and taciturn Host
Stands on the threshold, the wind
Shaking his thin white hairs —
Holds his lantern to scan
Our storm-beat figures, and asks:
Whom in our party we bring?
Whom we have left in the snow?

Sadly we answer: We bring
Only ourselves; we lost
Sight of the rest in the storm.
Hardly ourselves we fought through,
Stripp'd, without friends, as we are.
Friends, companions, and train
The avalanche swept from our side.

But thou would'st not *alone*
Be saved, my father! *alone*
Conquer and come to thy goal,
Leaving the rest in the wild.
We were weary, and we
Fearful, and we, in our march,
Fain to drop down and to die.
Still thou turnedst, and still
Beckonedst the trembler, and still
Gavest the weary thy hand!

If, in the paths of the world,
Stones might have wounded thy feet,
Toil or dejection have tried
Thy spirit, of that we saw
Nothing! to us thou wert still
Cheerful, and helpful, and firm.
Therefore to thee it was given
Many to save with thyself;
And, at the end of thy day,
O faithful shepherd! to come,
Bringing thy sheep in thy hand.

And through thee I believe
In the noble and great who are gone;
Pure souls honour'd and blest
By former ages, who else —
Such, so soulless, so poor,
Is the race of men whom I see —
Seem'd but a dream of the heart,
Seem'd but a cry of desire.
Yes! I believe that there lived
Others like thee in the past,
Not like the men of the crowd
Who all round me to-day
Bluster or cringe, and make life
Hideous, and arid, and vile;
But souls temper'd with fire,
Fervent, heroic, and good,
Helpers and friends of mankind.

Servants of God! — or sons
Shall I not call you? because
Not as servants ye knew
Your Father's innermost mind,
His, who unwillingly sees
One of his little ones lost —
Yours is the praise, if mankind
Hath not as yet in its march
Fainted, and fallen, and died!

See! in the rocks of the world
Marches the host of mankind,
A feeble, wavering line.
Where are they tending? — A God
Marshall'd them, gave them their goal. —
Ah, but the way is so long!
Years they have been in the wild!
Sore thirst plagues them; the rocks,
Rising all round, overawe.
Factions divide them; their host
Threatens to break, to dissolve.
Ah, keep, keep them combined!
Else, of the myriads who fill
That army, not one shall arrive!

Sole they shall stray; in the rocks
Labour for ever in vain,
Die one by one in the waste.

Then, in such hour of need
Of your fainting, dispirited race,
Ye, like angels, appear,
Radiant with ardour divine.
Beacons of hope, ye appear!
Languor is not in your heart,
Weakness is not in your word,
Weariness not on your brow.
Ye alight in our van; at your voice,
Panic, despair, flee away.
Ye move through the ranks, recall
The stragglers, refresh the outworn,
Praise, re-inspire the brave.
Order, courage, return.
Eyes rekindling, and prayers,
Follow your steps as ye go.
Ye fill up the gaps in our files,
Strengthen the wavering line,
Stablish, continue our march,
On, to the bound of the waste,
On, to the City of God.

The Last Word

Creep into thy narrow bed,
Creep, and let no more be said!
Vain thy onset! all stands fast;
Thou thyself must break at last.

Let the long contention cease!
Geese are swans and swans are geese.
Let them have it how they will!
Thou art tired; best be still!

They out-talk'd thee, hiss'd thee, tore thee.
Better men fared thus before thee;

Fired their ringing shot and pass'd,
Hotly charged — and broke at last.

Charge once more, then, and be dumb!
Let the victors, when they come,
When the forts of folly fall,
Find thy body by the wall.

Alphabetical List of Titles

Alphabetical List of First Lines

All books complete and unabridged. All 5³⁄₁₆″ × 8¼″, paperbound.
Just $1.00–$2.00 in U.S.A.

POETRY (continued)

FICTION

DOVER · THRIFT · EDITIONS

All books complete and unabridged. All 5³⁄₁₆″ × 8¼″, paperbound.
Just $1.00–$2.00 in U.S.A.

FICTION (continued)

THE MAN WHO WOULD BE KING AND OTHER STORIES, Rudyard Kipling. 128pp. 28051-9 $1.00

SELECTED SHORT STORIES, D. H. Lawrence. 128pp. 27794-1 $1.00

GREEN TEA AND OTHER GHOST STORIES, J. Sheridan LeFanu. 96pp. 27795-X $1.00

THE CALL OF THE WILD, Jack London. 64pp. 26472-6 $1.00

FIVE GREAT SHORT STORIES, Jack London. 96pp. 27063-7 $1.00

WHITE FANG, Jack London. 160pp. 26968-X $1.00

THE NECKLACE AND OTHER SHORT STORIES, Guy de Maupassant. 128pp. 27064-5 $1.00

BARTLEBY AND BENITO CERENO, Herman Melville. 112pp. 26473-4 $1.00

THE GOLD-BUG AND OTHER TALES, Edgar Allan Poe. 128pp. 26875-6 $1.00

THE QUEEN OF SPADES AND OTHER STORIES, Alexander Pushkin. 128pp. 28054-3 $1.00

THREE LIVES, Gertrude Stein. 176pp. 28059-4 $2.00

THE STRANGE CASE OF DR. JEKYLL AND MR. HYDE, Robert Louis Stevenson. 64pp. 26688-5 $1.00

TREASURE ISLAND, Robert Louis Stevenson. 160pp. 27559-0 $1.00

THE KREUTZER SONATA AND OTHER SHORT STORIES, Leo Tolstoy. 144pp. 27805-0 $1.00

ADVENTURES OF HUCKLEBERRY FINN, Mark Twain. 224pp. 28061-6 $2.00

THE MYSTERIOUS STRANGER AND OTHER STORIES, Mark Twain. 128pp. 27069-6 $1.00

CANDIDE, Voltaire (François-Marie Arouet). 112pp. 26689-3 $1.00

THE INVISIBLE MAN, H. G. Wells. 112pp. (Available in U.S. only.) 27071-8 $1.00

ETHAN FROME, Edith Wharton. 96pp. 26690-7 $1.00

THE PICTURE OF DORIAN GRAY, Oscar Wilde. 192pp. 27807-7 $1.00

NONFICTION

THE DEVIL'S DICTIONARY, Ambrose Bierce. 144pp. 27542-6 $1.00

THE SOULS OF BLACK FOLK, W. E. B. Du Bois. 176pp. 28041-1 $2.00

SELF-RELIANCE AND OTHER ESSAYS, Ralph Waldo Emerson. 128pp. 27790-9 $1.00

GREAT SPEECHES, Abraham Lincoln. 112pp. 26872-1 $1.00

THE PRINCE, Niccolò Machiavelli. 80pp. 27274-5 $1.00

SYMPOSIUM AND PHAEDRUS, Plato. 96pp. 27798-4 $1.00

THE TRIAL AND DEATH OF SOCRATES: FOUR DIALOGUES, Plato. 128pp. 27066-1 $1.00

CIVIL DISOBEDIENCE AND OTHER ESSAYS, Henry David Thoreau. 96pp. 27563-9 $1.00

THE THEORY OF THE LEISURE CLASS, Thorstein Veblen. 256pp. 28062-4 $2.00

PLAYS

THE CHERRY ORCHARD, Anton Chekhov. 64pp. 26682-6 $1.00

THE THREE SISTERS, Anton Chekhov. 64pp. 27544-2 $1.00

THE WAY OF THE WORLD, William Congreve. 80pp. 27787-9 $1.00

MEDEA, Euripides. 64pp. 27548-5 $1.00

THE MIKADO, William Schwenck Gilbert. 64pp. 27268-0 $1.00